This book belongs to:

Sketch your World

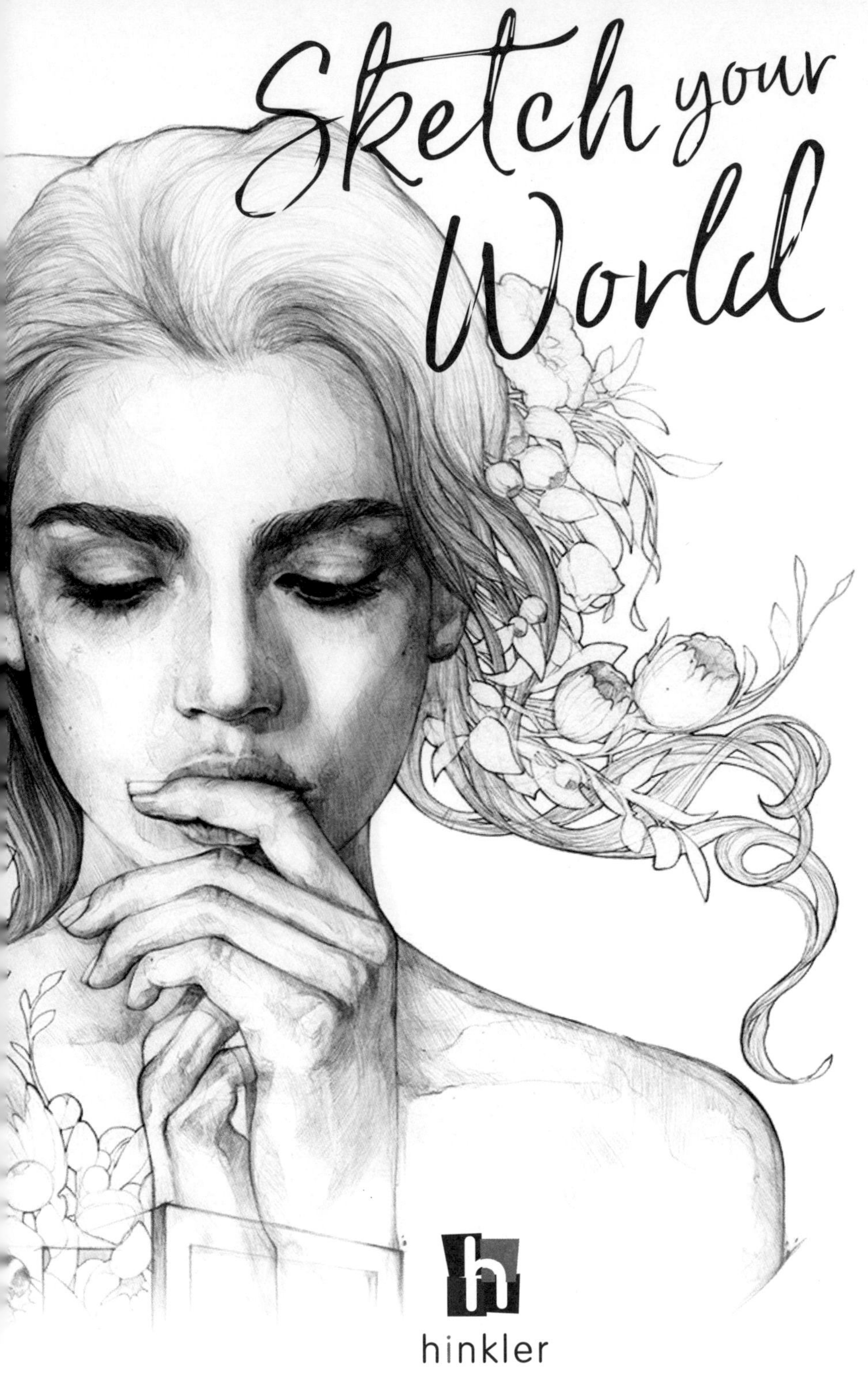

hinkler

Published by Hinkler Books Pty Ltd
45–55 Fairchild Street
Heatherton Victoria 3202 Australia
www.hinkler.com

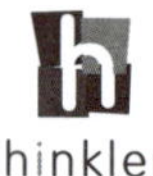

Text and illustrations pp4-5; 7-21: Priscilla Heywood
Text and illustrations p6: Michelle Zuccolo
People Illustrations p1; pp24-25: Dmitry Pogorelov
Animal illustrations pp44-45: Okan Bulbul
Places illustrations pp70-71: Carol Robinson
Still Life illustrations pp94-95: Carol Robinson
Doodles illustrations pp118-119: Gabi Murphy
Internal design: CB Design
Prepress: Splitting Image

ISBN 9781 4889 41108

Printed and bound in Malaysia

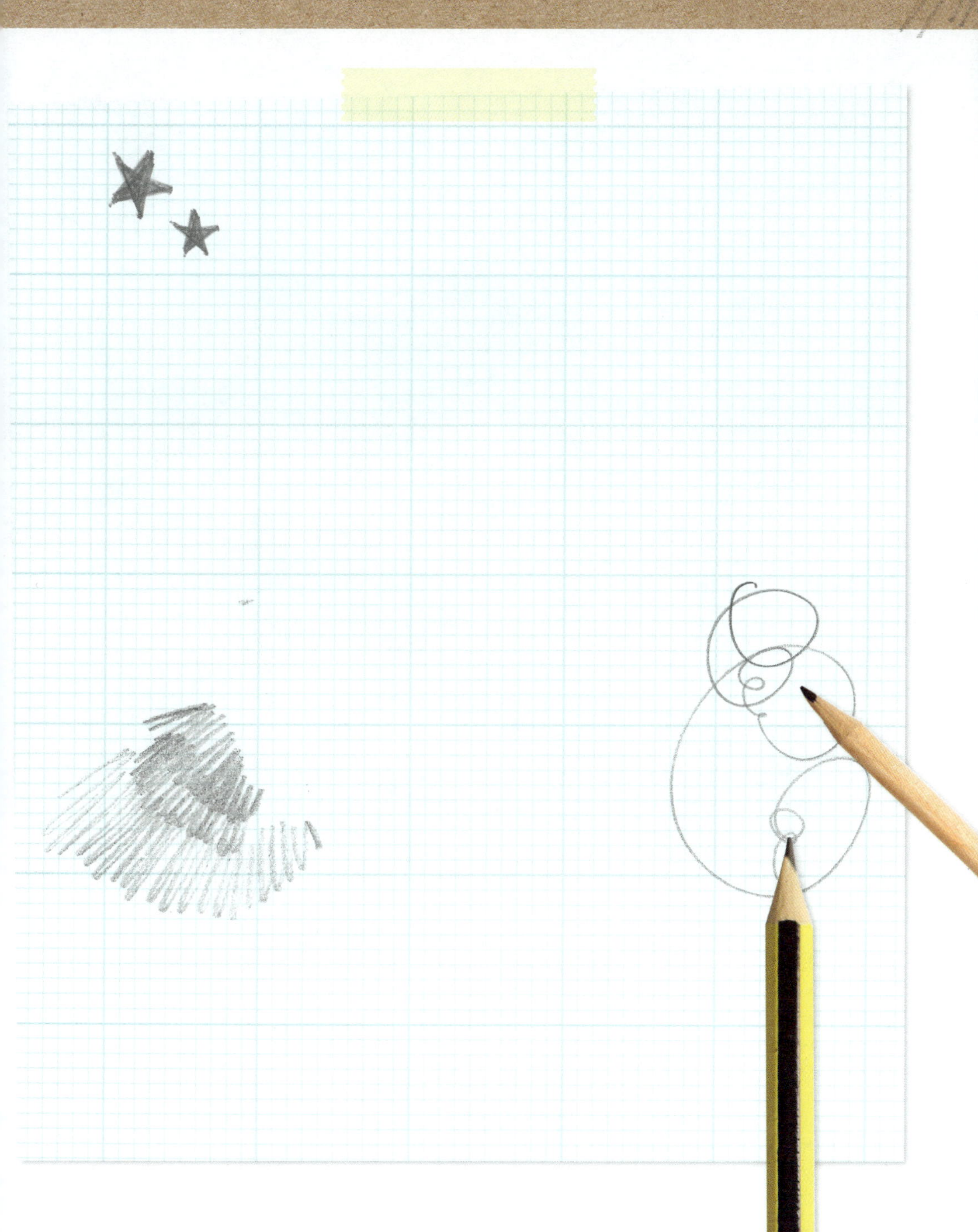

Hand positions

THE TWO MAIN POSITIONS ARE:

HANDWRITING POSITION
This can be used for precision lines and careful application of tone and accents.

UNDERHAND POSITION
In this hold, the pencil passes under the hand instead of over the thumb. It's great for looser lines and strokes and helps to free up your work. This is a great position for quickly sketching in large works.

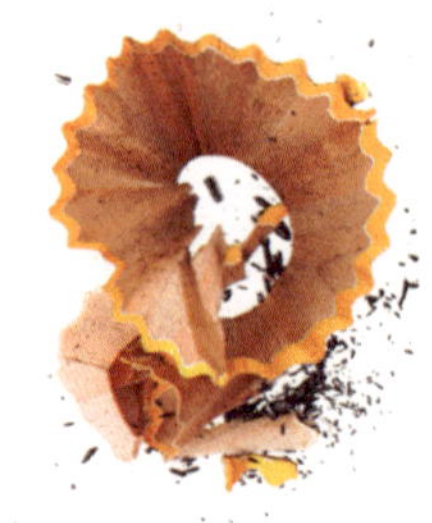

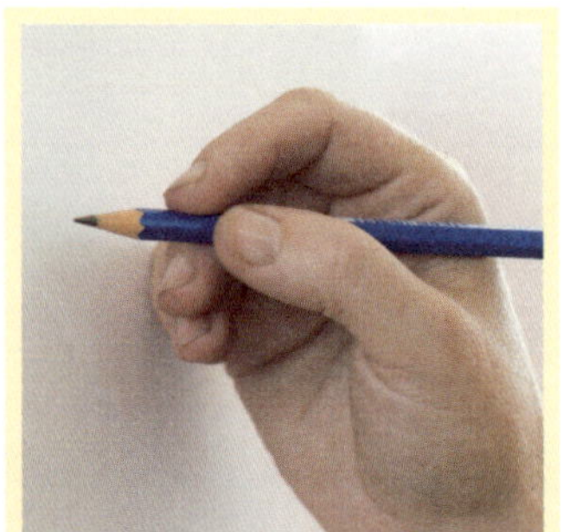

Handwriting position

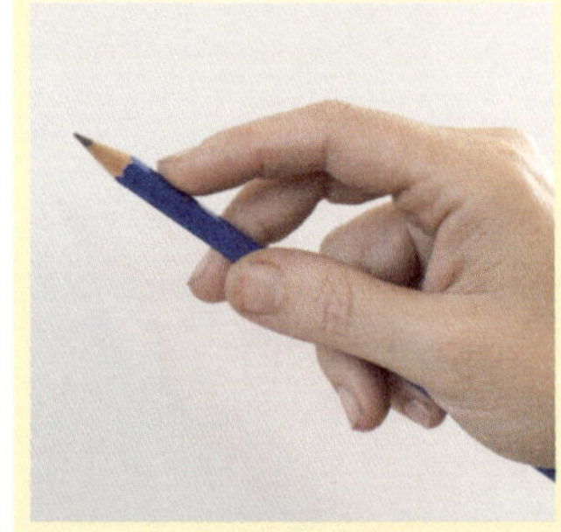

Underhand position

OTHER HAND POSITIONS

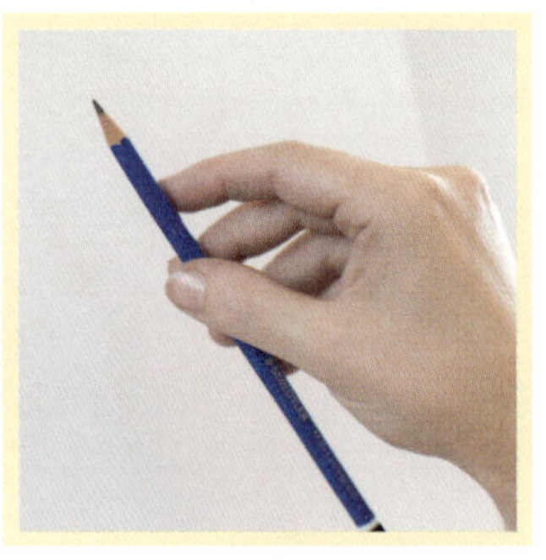

Cupped hand position

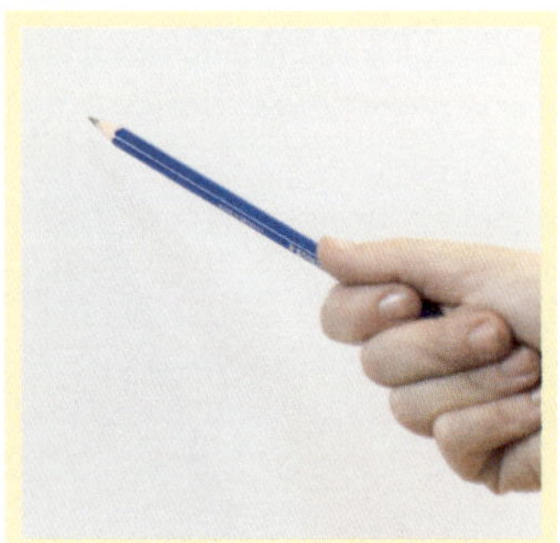

Pencil on the side position

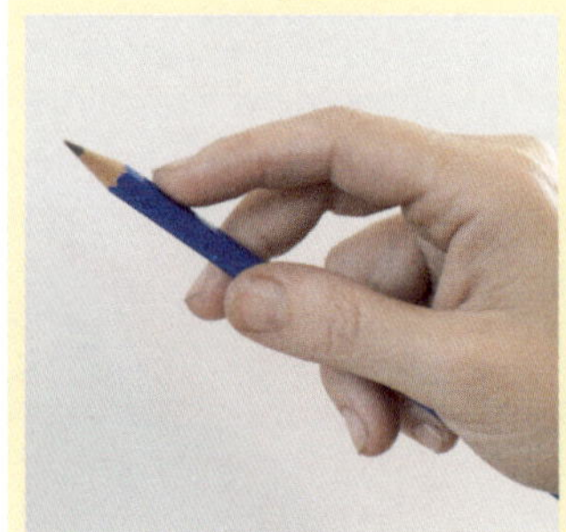

Fencing foil position

There are many other ways to hold your pencil. The 'cupped hand' position is similar to the underhand position, but the whole hand turns around so that the palm faces up. The 'pencil on the side' position is the opposite and has the top of the hand facing up and the pencil held loosely in the fingers, not touching the hand at all. There's also the 'fencing foil' position, which has the fingers curled around the pencil like a sword.

Have fun changing positions, but focus on the main two in the beginning. The important thing is to make sure you're relaxed when you hold the pencil and that it feels comfortable and natural.

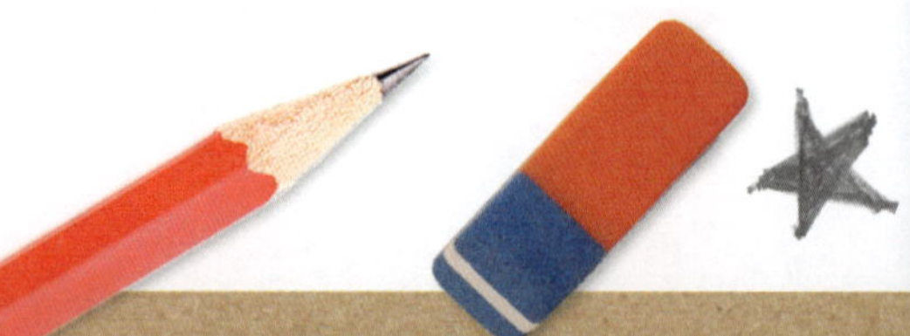

Experiments with pencil

VARIATIONS WITH LINE, TEXTURE AND TONE

Practise drawing straight lines freehand and then circular strokes followed by scribbles and flicked lines. See if you can create thick lines and thin lines with all the different types of leads. Also experiment with the different lines produced when your pencil is sharp and blunt. Try using the different leads laid flat to create a smooth result. Try it now on the tip of the pencil.

The following examples show a number of different ways to create texture. Even the most experienced artists are always experimenting with different ways to use the pencil.

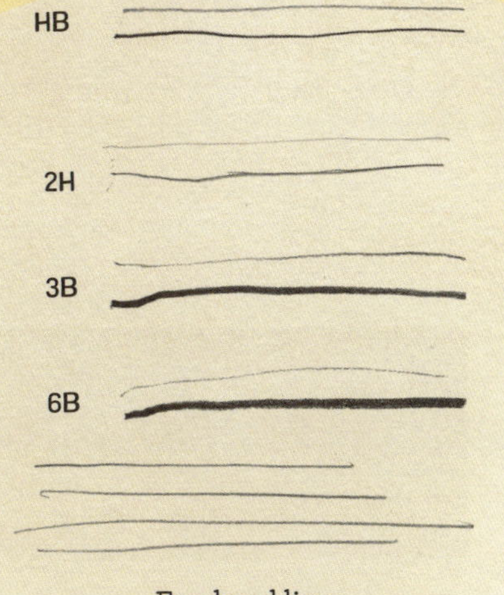

Freehand lines

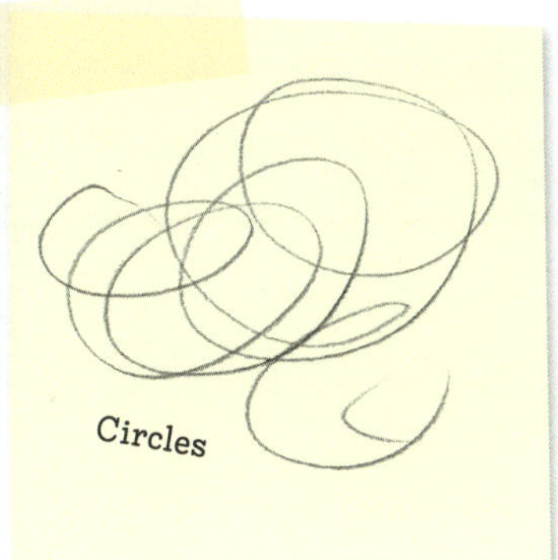
Circles

Directional scribbles 2H

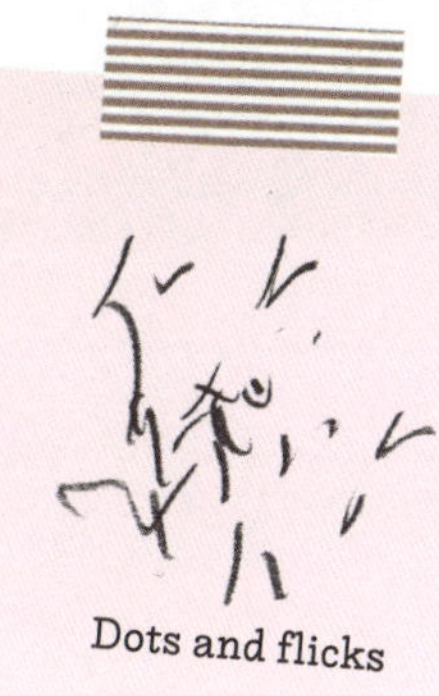
Dots and flicks

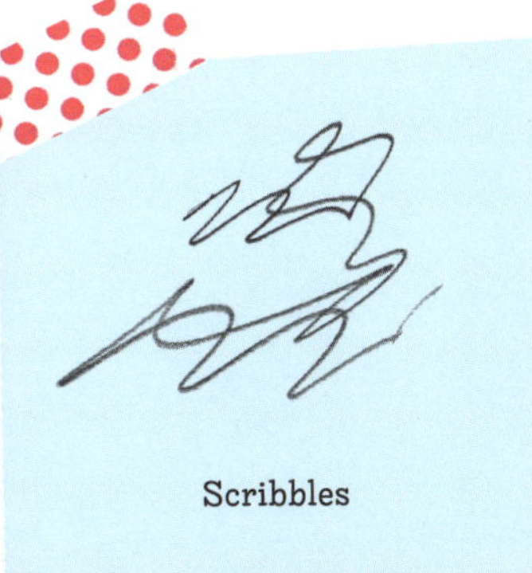
Scribbles

Directional scribbles 4B

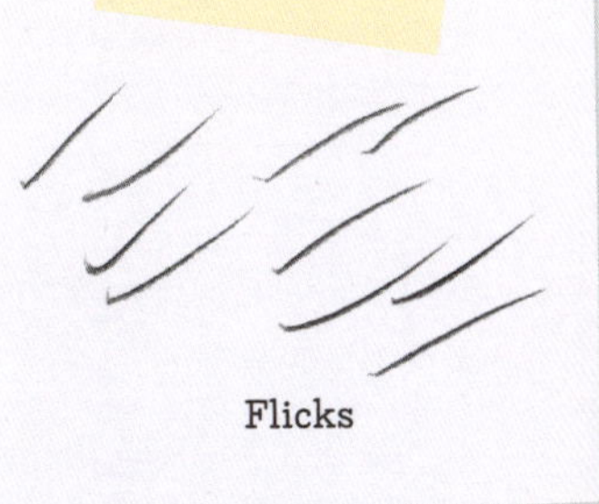
Flicks

Hatching and crosshatching

These techniques are really useful for creating tone. Hatching is simply closely packed straight lines in a diagonal direction.

Crosshatching is when lines are laid over the top in the opposite direction and then vertically and horizontally as well. This can create a really smooth effect.

Using crosshatching, try to create a scale of tone using an HB pencil like the following example. You can follow this up with a scale that has no separations.

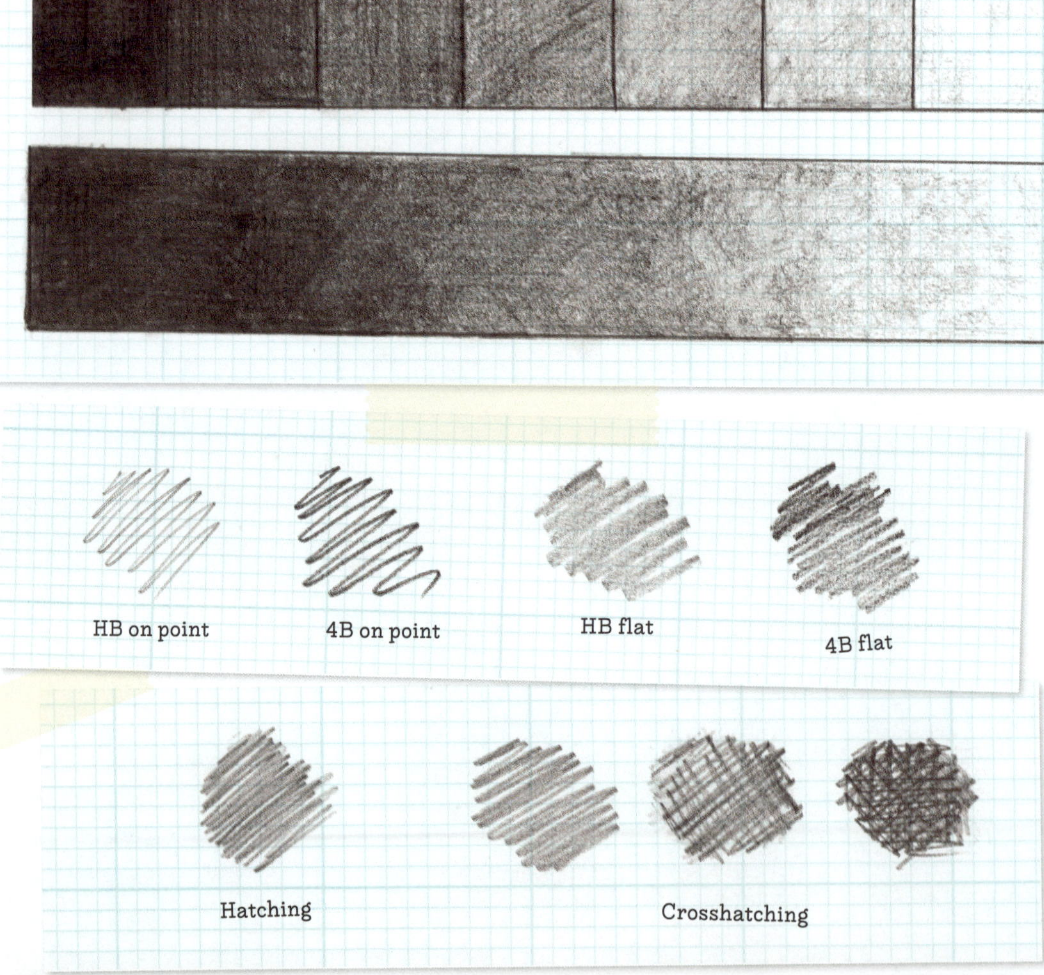

Sketching with fine-liner and brush-tip pens

When working with brush-tip pens, different types of paper can produce very different results. The type of paper and surface you work with will determine the marks your pen can make and create a variety of effects. Lines will be easier to control on smooth papers, and will bleed on others. Explore and have fun with these unique effects!

WHAT TO EXPECT

Ink pens characteristically produce dense black lines that create a striking contrast on white paper. Various techniques can be developed that allow you to replicate graduations, tonal variations and shadows. These create the illusion of more three-dimensional, convincing sketches.

FINE-LINER PENS

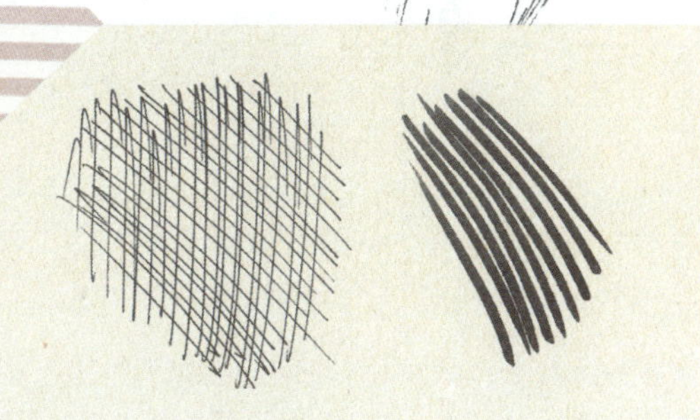

Fine-liner pens create a straightforward line that varies in width according to the size and shape of its head. A soft tip pen can be very flexible, producing thick marks, whereas thinner tips produce a decisive, narrow line.

BRUSH-TIP PENS

Holding a brush-tip pen in different ways can create different types of marks. With brush-tip pens, the initial mark can be thin and pointy. If you roll the pen on the page in a circular motion, however, you can create different, spiralling effects. With added speed and pressure, your lines can swell and recede, producing interesting

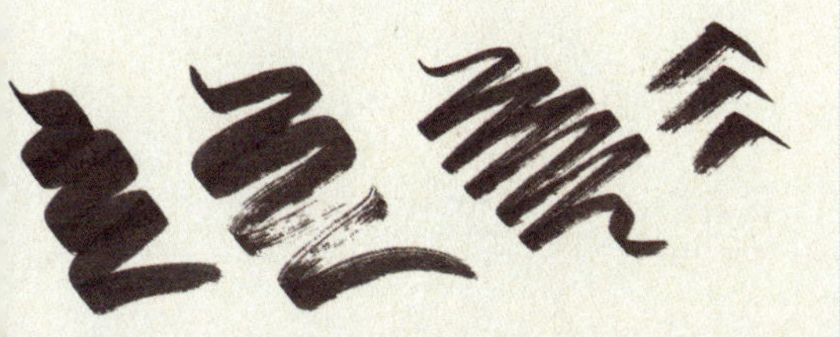

PREVENTING SMUDGES

After applying marks with pens, allow time for the ink to dry before you touch it. If using a ruler for parts of your drawing, remember that ink residue will remain on the edge of the equipment. Wipe this off on towelling paper to prevent smudges on reuse of the ruler.

TIP FOR SHADOWS

With a brush-tip pen, by applying thick, flat lines side by side, an impression of a flat, solid shadow can be created. If working with fine-liners, another approach is to apply crosshatching lines at the base of the object you're sketching to create a shadow.

Three dimensions

Four basic shapes – the square, rectangle, triangle and circle – can be turned into three-dimensional objects with the illusion of line.

Starting with the square, you can add short lines of equal length to three of the corners. Make sure they are parallel and at about 45 degrees. Join those lines and you have a cube.

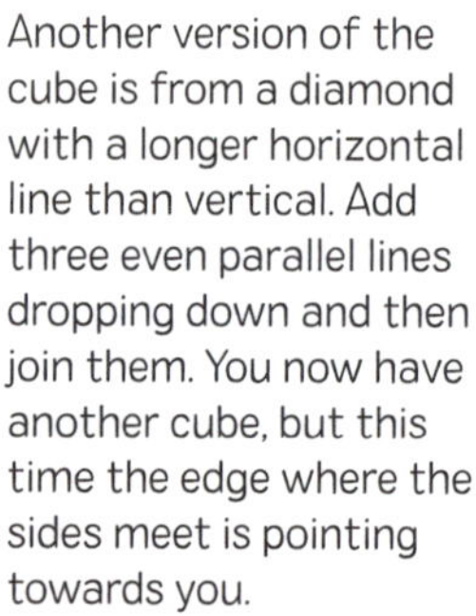

Another version of the cube is from a diamond with a longer horizontal line than vertical. Add three even parallel lines dropping down and then join them. You now have another cube, but this time the edge where the sides meet is pointing towards you.

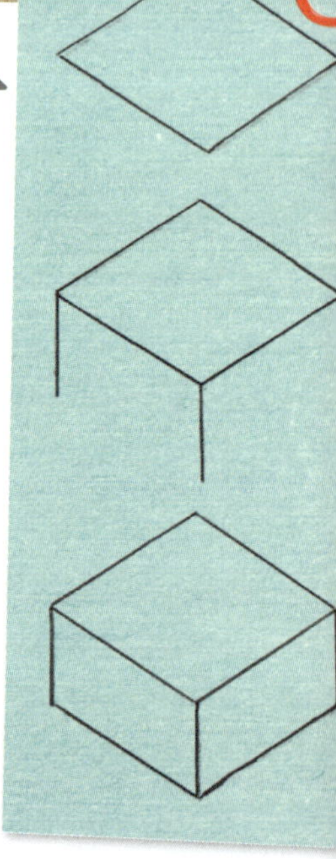

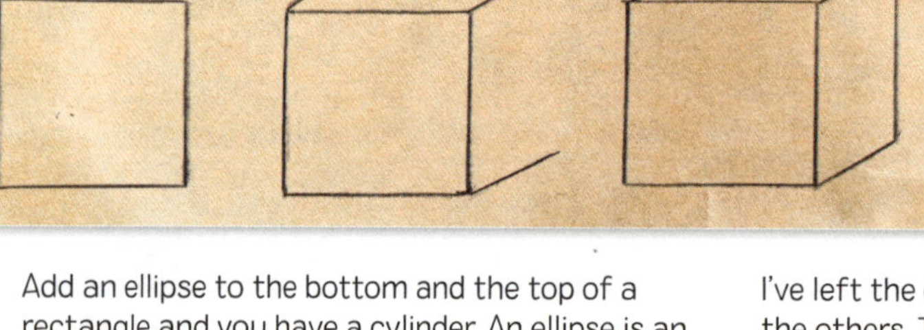

Add an ellipse to the bottom and the top of a rectangle and you have a cylinder. An ellipse is an oval shape and each quarter is the same shape and size. The best way to draw it accurately is simply through practice and using your eye to see if it looks right.

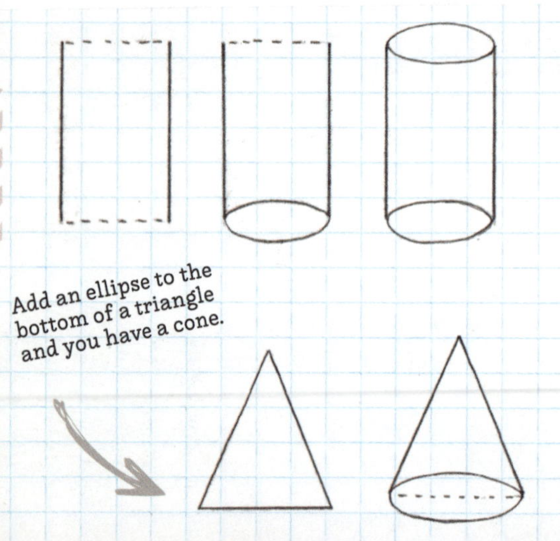

Add an ellipse to the bottom of a triangle and you have a cone.

I've left the circle to last as it's a little different to the others. To turn a circle into a sphere, you don't need to add any lines, but simply shading.

Start by drawing a circle and lightly shade it, leaving a white spot in the upper left corner. Make sure the shading is gradual and that the light spot is noticeably lighter. To add to the effect, fade a soft shadow away from the light side under the circle.

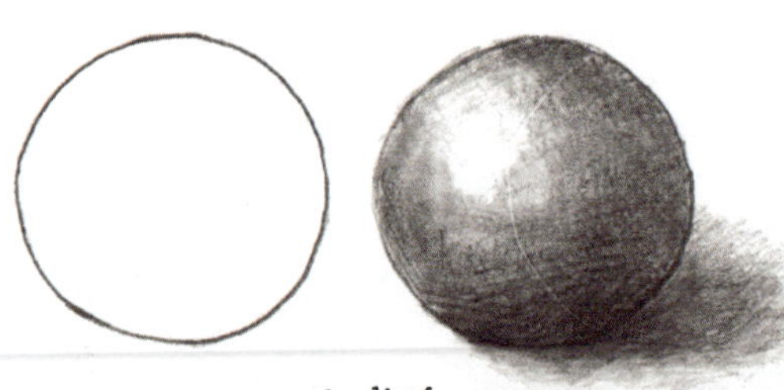

Now have a go at shading the other shapes as well.

Seeing the basic shapes in objects

Basic shapes can be seen in all objects around us. Sometimes they are simple and easy to recognise, like the cube in a cardboard box, and sometimes they are more complex and are made up of many shapes, taking a practiced eye to see.

We're going to start with simple objects where one basic shape is easy to see, such as a chess piece that is the shape of a cone.

1. Start by drawing a cone with an HB pencil. Sketch it in lightly so you can make changes without leaving any permanent marks.
2. Next, start adding the shape of the chess piece around the cone.
3. Finish off by adding small amounts of tone using the 3B and smooth it out with a 2H over the top, or use a paper stump for a more polished effect.

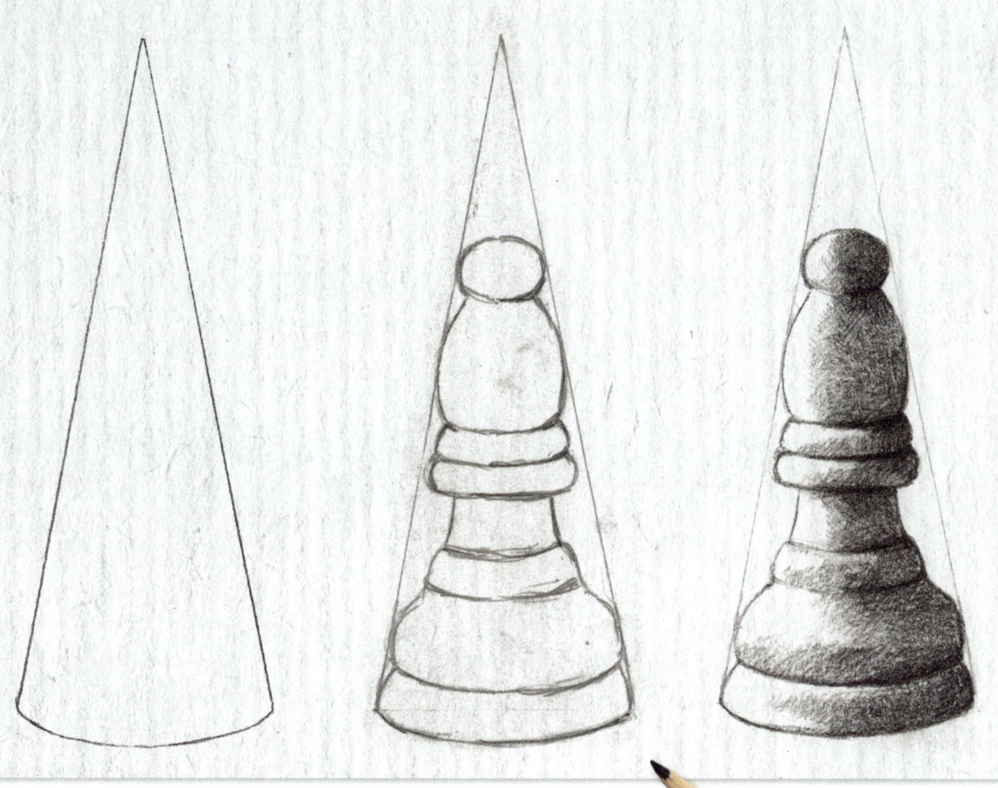

Have a look around the house and see what else you can find that fits a basic shape. It could be a clock, a camera, a long glass, a log of wood or a basketball. Have a go at drawing these following the same steps.

Perspective

Perspective is a fabulous tool to aid our 3D effect. Have you ever noticed how a road looks smaller as it goes into the distance and seems to vanish? That is an example of perspective.

ONE-POINT PERSPECTIVE

The horizon line is either the actual horizon or whatever horizontal line is level with your eye. When two parallel lines recede into the distance, they converge towards a point. This is called the vanishing point. The following drawing demonstrates this. All the lines meet at one point.

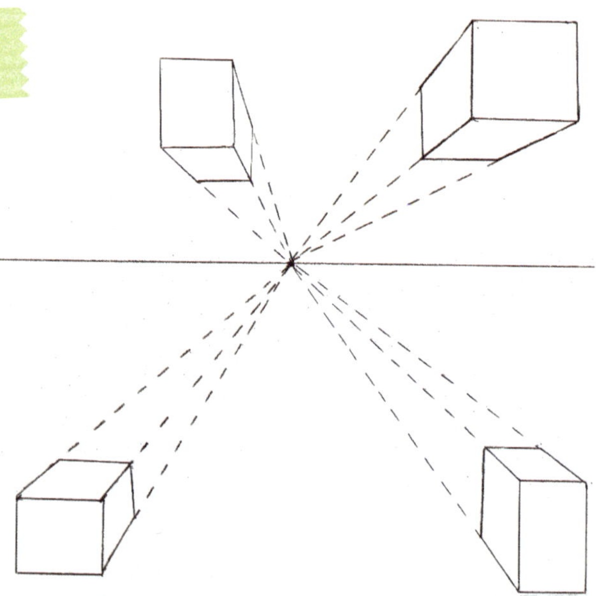

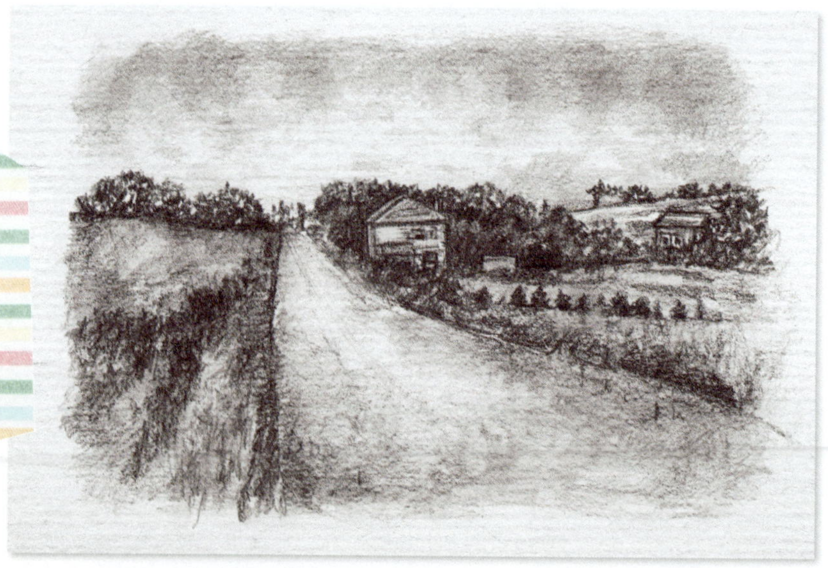

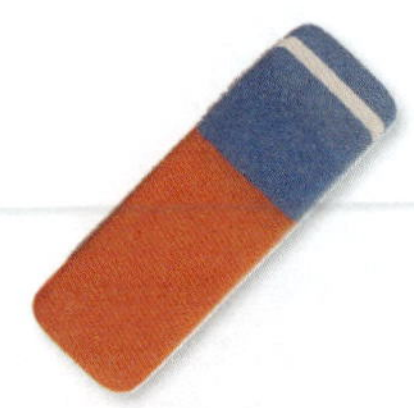

TWO-POINT PERSPECTIVE

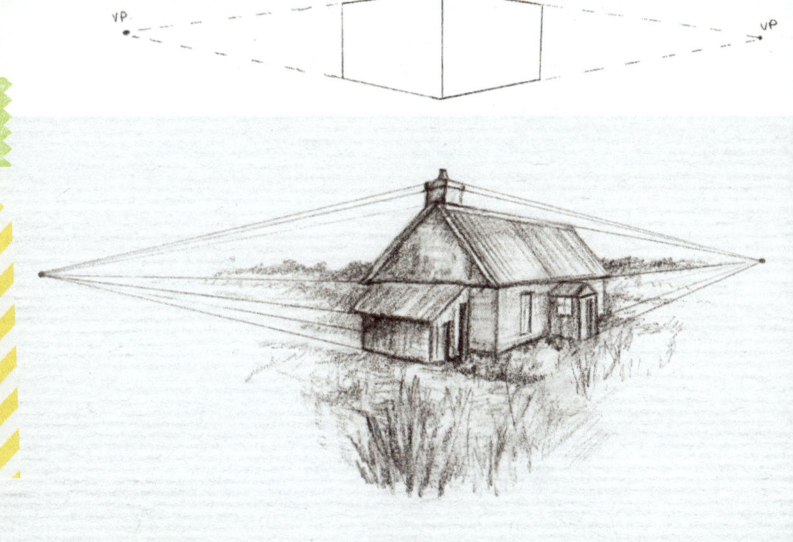

When an object isn't at a full frontal view, you will see two sides or planes. This will then have two vanishing points: one to the left and one to the right. This can also apply to

THREE-POINT PERSPECTIVE

If the object is viewed from an extreme angle, the vertical lines have their own vanishing point as well. This is used when you're viewing something from a very low or high point.

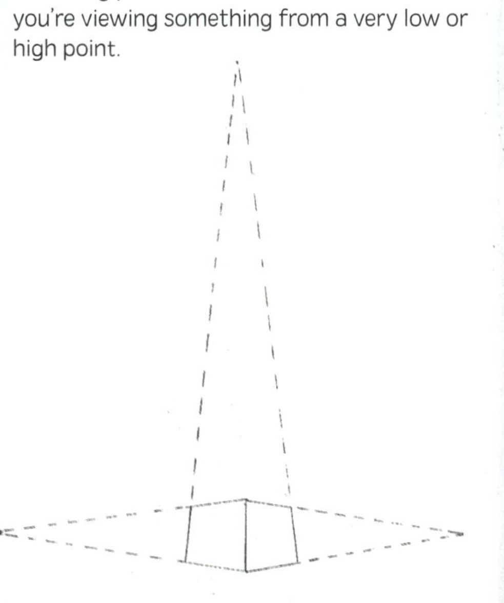

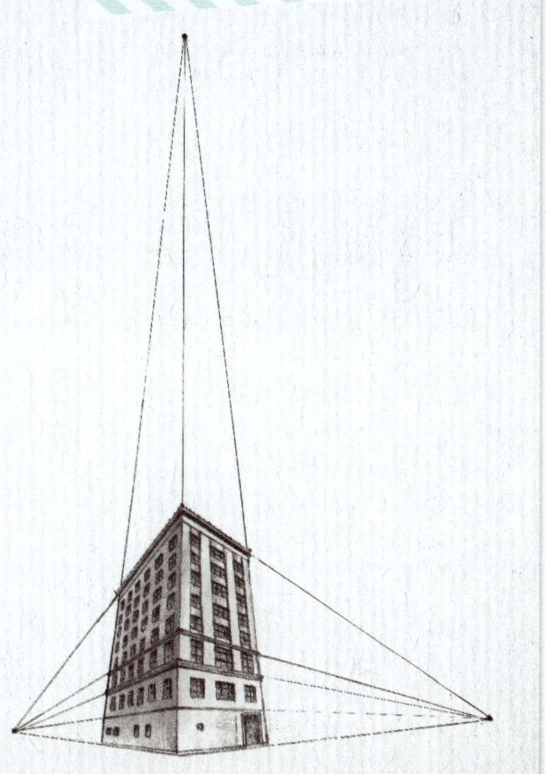

The human form

The human form can be one of the most interesting subjects to draw. When drawing figures, it's useful to have some idea of the structure of the body. In Leonardo da Vinci's day, they used to dissect the body to analyse how it works. We don't need to do that, but it does help to have some idea of proportions.

It's generally accepted that the length of the head will fit seven-and-a-half times into the body. The classical proportions were eight heads to the length of the body, but many of the figures drawn in that time were god-like figures. Although this is still used today for fashion drawings and magazines, the more realistic proportions are seven-and-a-half heads to the length of the body.

The midpoint of the body is at the pubic bone, not at the waist as many people think.

The female form is more rounded with narrower shoulders and wider hips than the male.

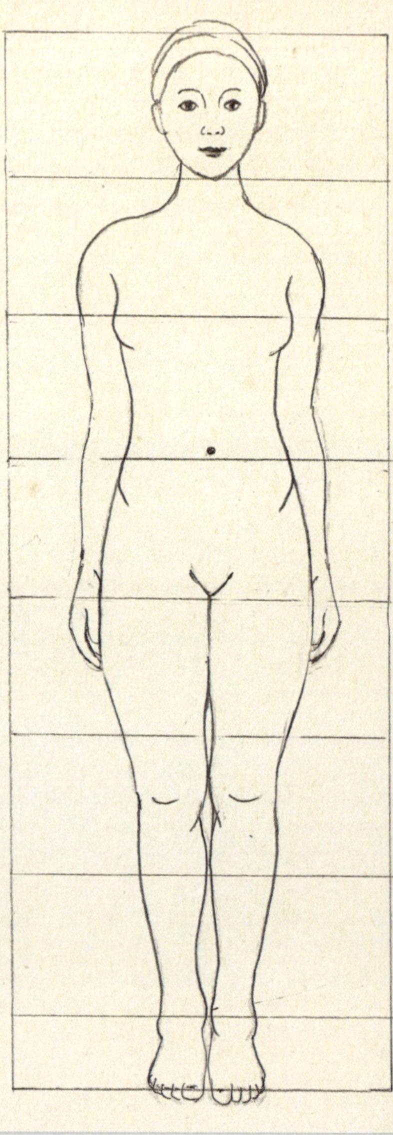

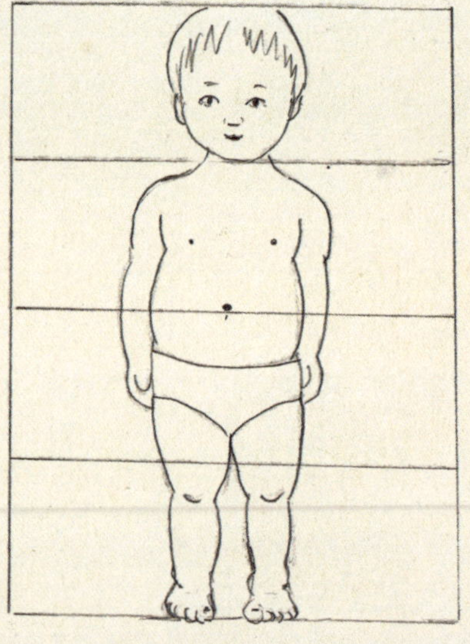

Children have slightly different proportions to adults. Toddlers are approximately four heads tall and six- to seven-year-old children are six heads tall. By the age of ten, they are about seven heads tall.

WHEN THE HEAD IS VIEWED STRAIGHT ON:

★ The width of the head is about two-thirds of the height

★ The eyes are halfway between the top of the head and the chin

★ The bottom of the nose is halfway between the eyes and the chin

★ The bottom of the mouth is halfway between the nose and the chin

★ The corners of the mouth align with the centre of the eyes

★ The top of the ears align with the eyebrows

★ The bottom of the ears align with the bottom of the nose

★ The nose is the same width as the eyes

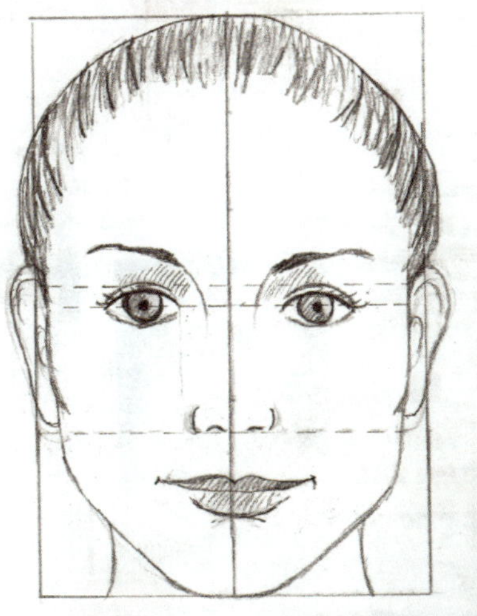

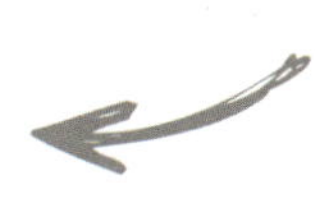

With the face in profile, the head divides in half at the jawline in front of the ears. The back of the head is deceptively larger than many people think. The only part that projects beyond this is the nose, which can be variable in size.

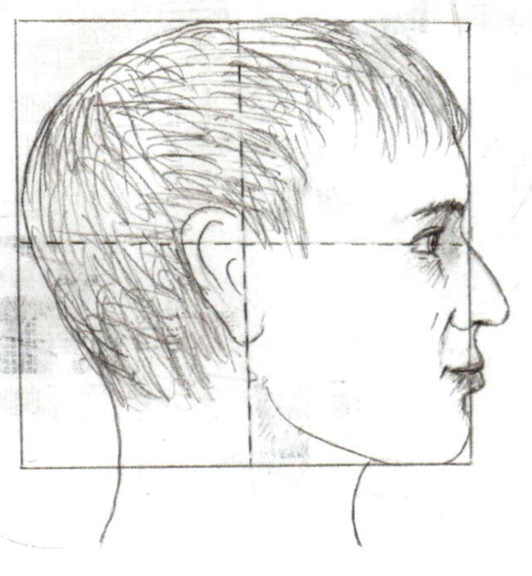

Children and babies have a proportionally larger forehead. With a baby, you'll find the middle of the eyes is three-sevenths up the face. The lower lip is on the first seventh and the nose is on the next.

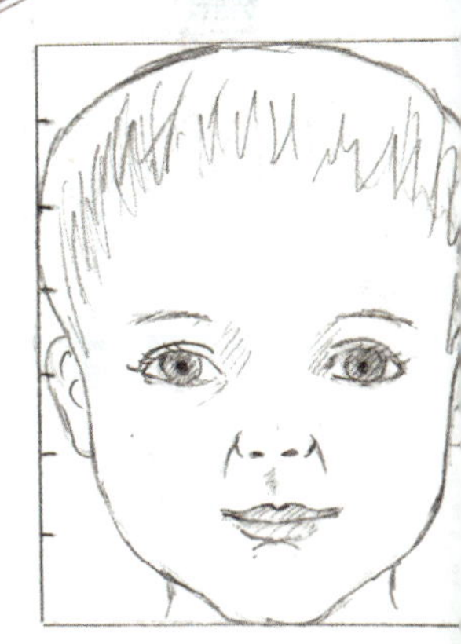

These are, of course, generalisations and with all these proportions and characteristics, it's important to double-check what you're drawing from your model and reference. Check if it really is what you're seeing, especially once you start drawing heads from all sorts of angles. When foreshortening distorts proportions, your eye is the best tool you have.

CHARACTERISTICS AND EXPRESSIONS

THE FACE FRONT ON

The lips have two peaks and a dent on the upper lip under the nose. The line where the lips meet should mostly be a darker line than the outside of the lips. Only part of the ears can be seen. And although it may seem silly, don't forget to draw the eyelids if they're visible. Many beginners forget that we have eyelids and compensate with really big eyelashes.

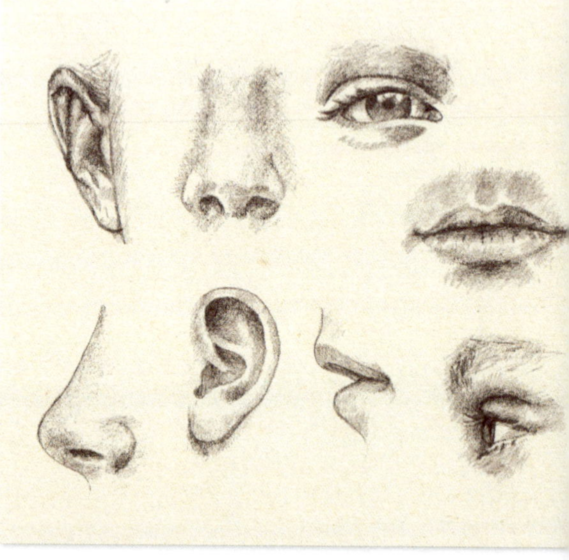

THE FACE IN PROFILE

The eyes in profile are a completely different shape to when they are viewed front on and look roughly similar to a triangle. The mouth is half the length, so make sure you don't draw it too long. The eyes do not go above the nose in profile. This is a common mistake.

THE FACE IN THREE-QUARTER VIEW

When drawing the face at three-quarter view, the eye further away will be a different shape and will appear much shorter. The half of the mouth furthest away will also be smaller, as will part of the nose.

Drawing different expressions can be one of the most enjoyable drawing experiences. Everyone can connect with human emotions, so immediately you're creating something your viewing audience will relate to.

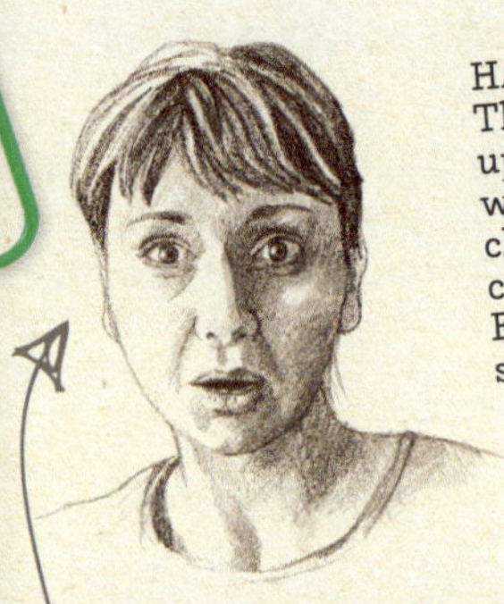

SHOCKED
The eyes are wide and staring with the whole iris visible. Wrinkles will often appear in the forehead from raised eyebrows and the mouth will be open loosely.

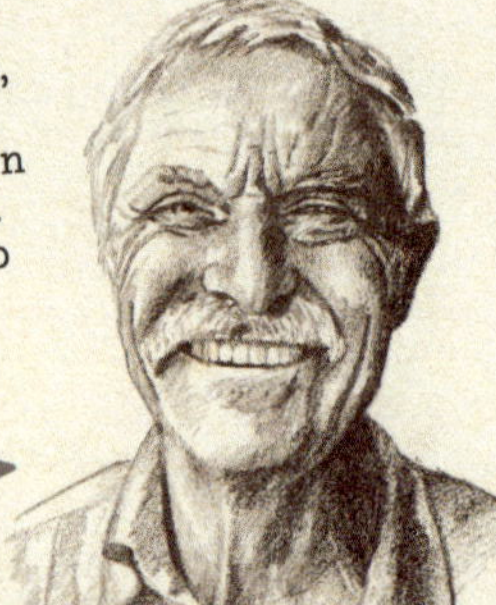

HAPPY
The mouth turns up, showing teeth, which raises the cheeks and in turn crinkles the eyes. Eyebrows tend to stay neutral.

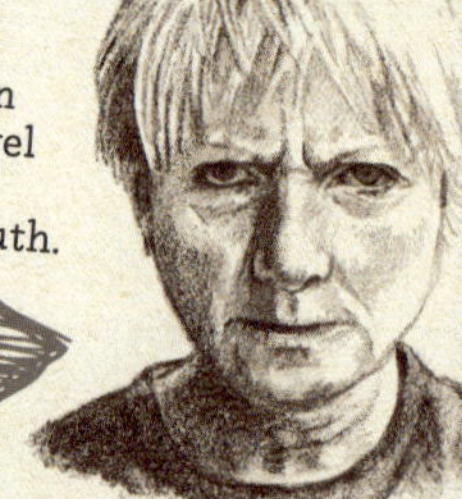

ANGRY
The eyes will be narrowed with the brows drawn together causing frown lines. The mouth turns down and lines will travel down from the corners of the mouth.

There are a whole multitude of different expressions for you to explore. Search different expressions on the internet and see what common characteristics you can find, or ask your friends and family to pull faces for you.

HANDS AND FEET

A lot of people avoid hands and feet, thinking that they're harder than everything else. They're not. You just need to break them down into simple elements and practise drawing them.

The middle finger on our hands is only slightly shorter than the length of the palm. Our whole hand is as long as the length from our chin to near the top of our forehead. People often make the mistake of drawing hands too small.

The best way to get used to drawing hands is to practise in as many different positions as possible. Always mark in the knuckles, as they give the bends and contours.

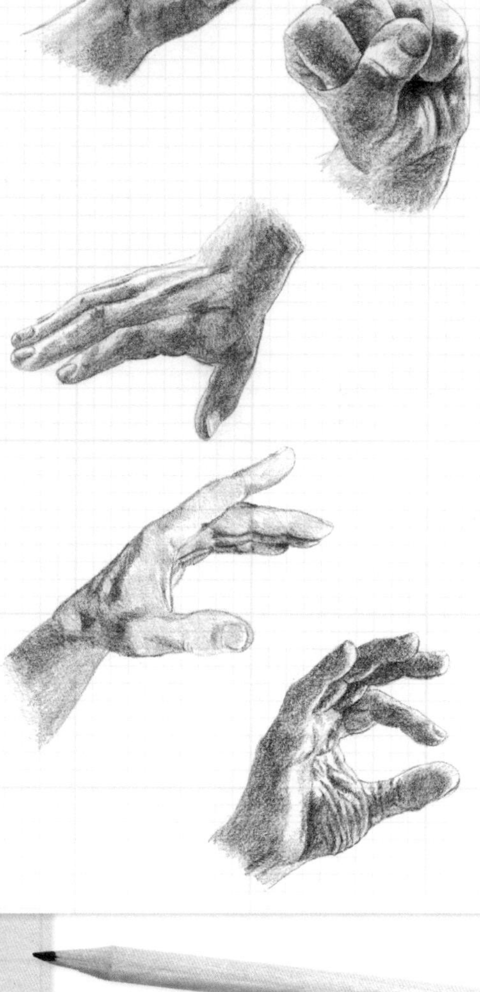

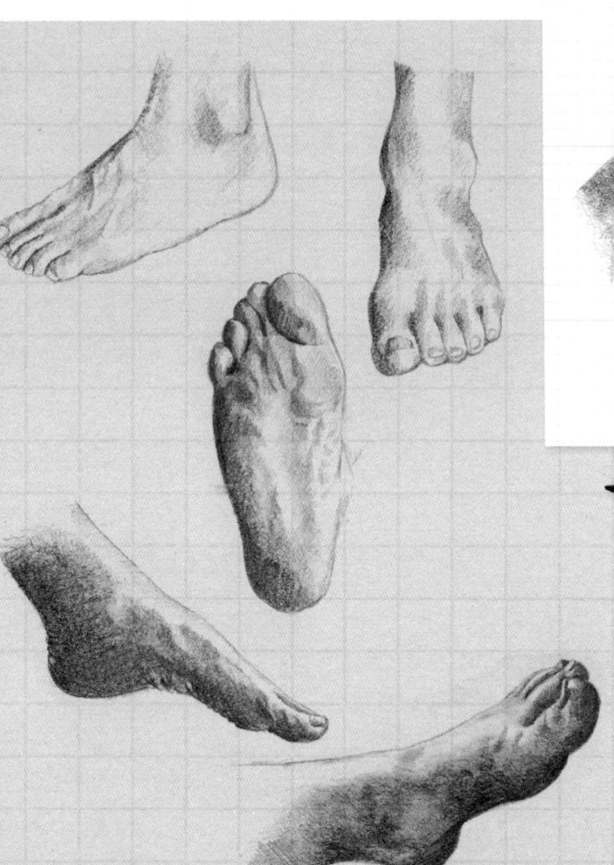

The feet are approximately the size of our head. The ankle bone is larger on the outside of the foot than the inside and these bones are important in making the foot look real. The large toe goes into the rest of the foot about four times and, of course, the other toes get smaller.

GESTURE DRAWING

These are super-quick drawings with the aim being to catch the movement of the pose. They're great for training the eye to draw action and become familiar with the body in all its angles.

Start with a stick figure to capture the basic pose and movement. Then begin to flesh it out. Use quick sketchy lines to find where the line should lie. This can also create the illusion of movement. Don't spend longer than five minutes on any drawing.

Try drawing on location with your visual diary and capturing the people passing by. Sporting events can be great. Or if you're sitting at a café, drawing while enjoying coffee and cake is a fabulous way to spend the afternoon!

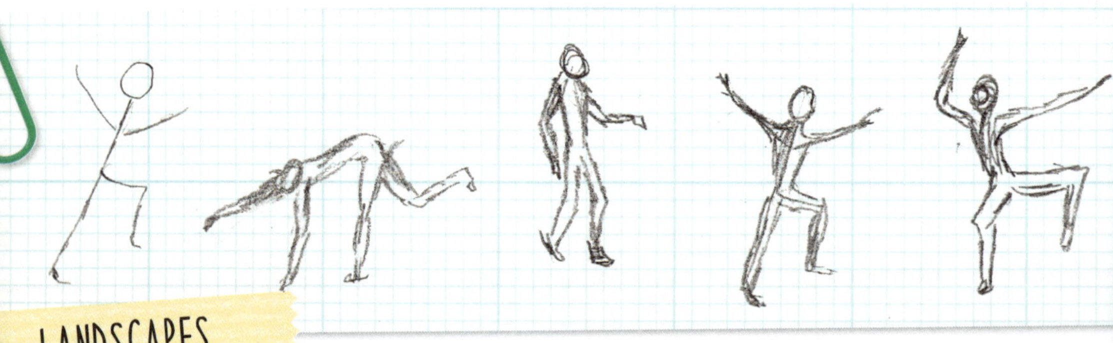

LANDSCAPES

There's a whole world out there waiting for you to draw it. You may see fantastic landscapes when you are travelling, but sometimes amazing landscapes can be just outside your front door if you look around. They can be the beach, a lovely park, or even the haphazard towers of the city.

Drawing landscapes is great for developing your compositional skills. One particular scene can often be broken down into a number of different possibilities and you have the exciting job of deciding which one you'd like.

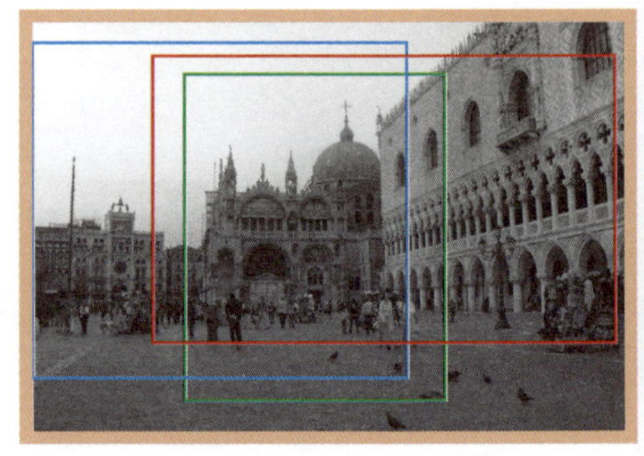

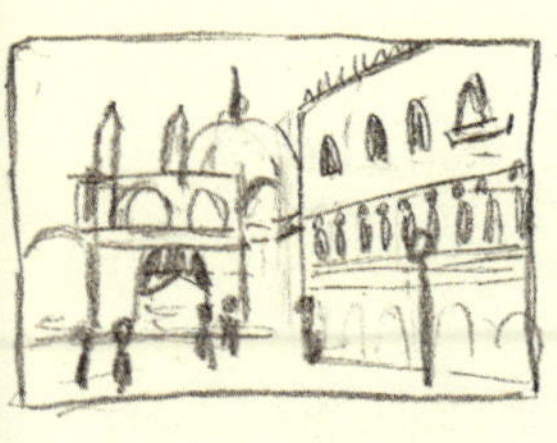

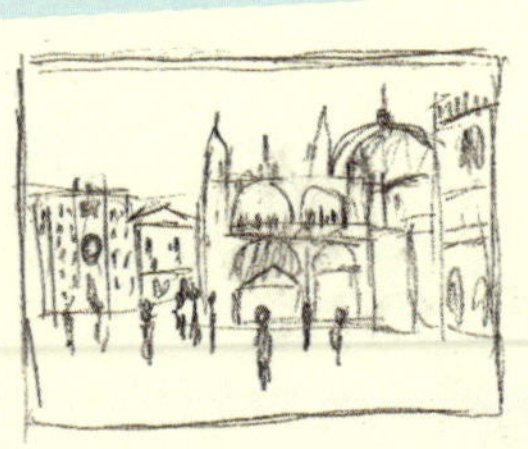

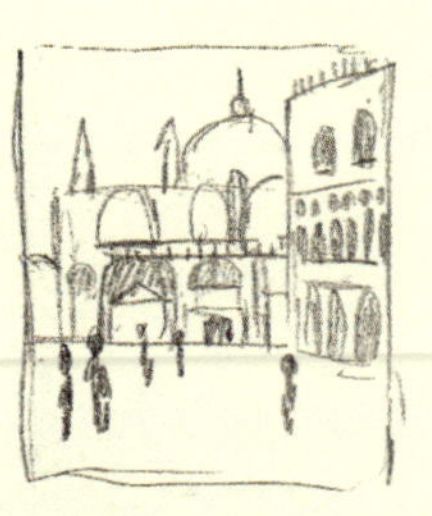

Creating frames, like above, is great in this sort of situation and helps you to play around with a whole gamut of compositions. Drawing quick thumbnails is helpful in finalising your decision as to what works best.

THE NATURAL LANDSCAPE

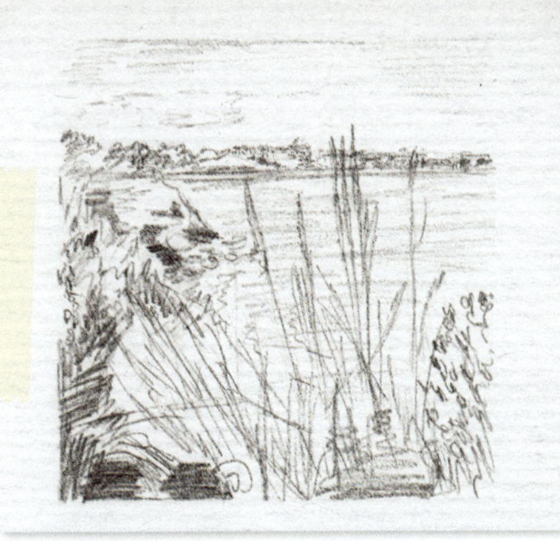

Choose a time of day that suits the mood you are after. Late in the afternoon near sunset provides a lovely soft light with interesting long shadows.

Lightly sketch it first, making sure your marks are light enough to change if need be. The great thing about a landscape is that you can be a little looser with the proportions. Nobody will know if the tree you're drawing is bigger than it actually is. As long as it makes sense altogether, that's the main thing.

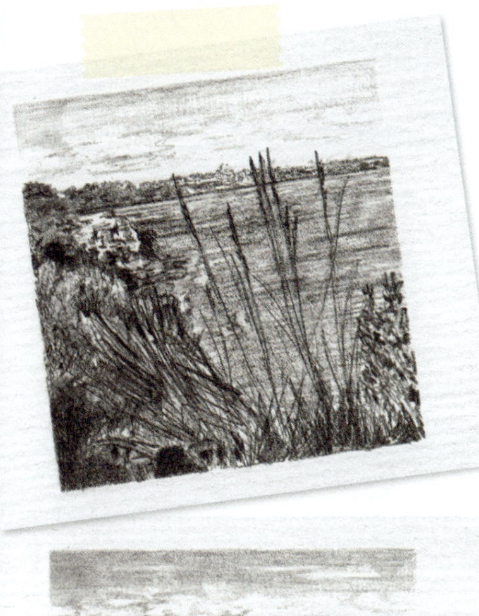

The branches in the foreground help break up the composition and, by having the larger object towards the front, give depth to everything else. The landscape becomes smaller, receding into the distance.

Next you can add in more detail. When drawing trees, you don't have to draw in every leaf. In fact it will look forced if you do. Look at the general pattern that the trees make and imitate that. Each type of tree will have its own pattern in how the leaves group together. Some may need squiggles to create the effect; some may need flicks. Most trees have gaps in the foliage where the sky shows through. Just as if you were drawing an object, start to add in tone. Notice how the trees have dark and light patches. Sometimes people get so caught up in drawing the detail on trees they forget to shade these variations and the trees lose form.

As they recede, landscapes often become lighter and the atmosphere is less distinct. Use your tone to show this and make it blurrier as it goes back with less defined lines. This will add to the depth of your drawing.

Enhance the depth and dark tones using a full range of pencils. Pick out the highlights with your kneadable eraser and use the paper stump on the blurrier bits in the background.

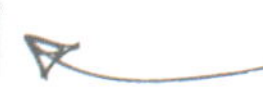

With a sharp pencil, redefine the foreground objects, making sure they're sharply in focus.

THE URBAN LANDSCAPE

Urban landscapes have a real diversity of moods. They can be fast and manic, or detailed in architecture and form. They're great for developing your perspective skills and, as most buildings have square shapes and blocks, it's easy to apply the rules you have learnt.

With this landscape, block in the basic sha of the landscape, drawing it first as squar and shapes so you can check that the perspective is correct.

Once satisfied, you can start to add the detail, with windows and trimming on the buildings and cars.

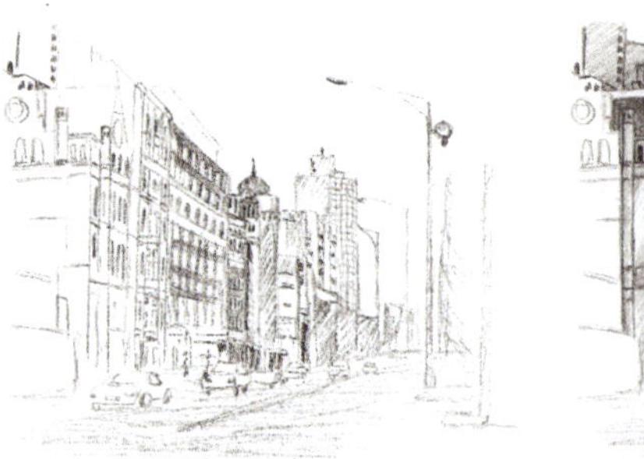

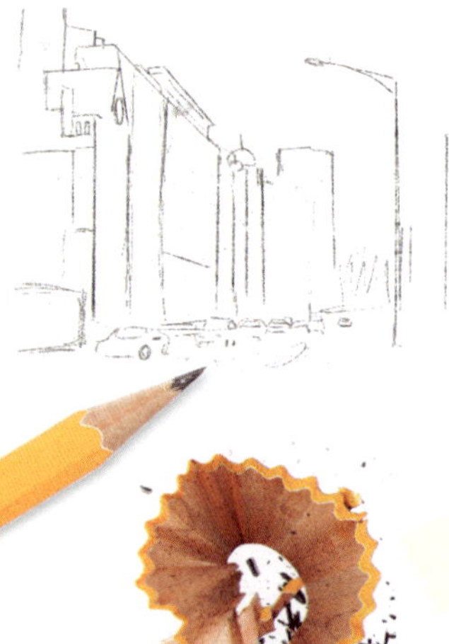

Finally add tone and build up the detail again where it may have become lost when you shaded in the highlights and lowlights. Using a sharp pencil, pull out the detail on the foreground buildings and soften the detail on the buildings in the distance with a paper stump.

To make an urban landscape fascinating for the viewer, pay attention to detail. The more of the tiny nooks and crevices you put in, the better.

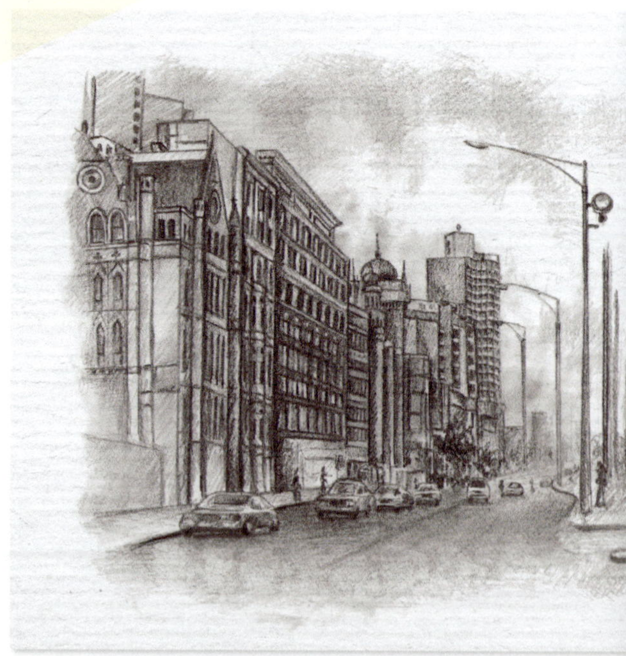

Animals

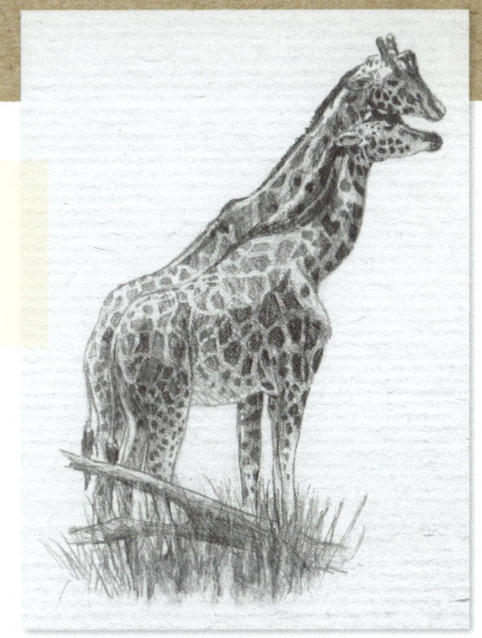

Drawing animals uses exactly the same skills and principles as we've used for all the other subjects. Measurement skills are particularly important, as the viewer will know if the proportions are incorrect more than they would with a generic vase.

Becoming familiar with the anatomy of various animals can be helpful. But the best thing is observation. Try drawing your family pet, or visit your friends and draw their pet as a present for them.

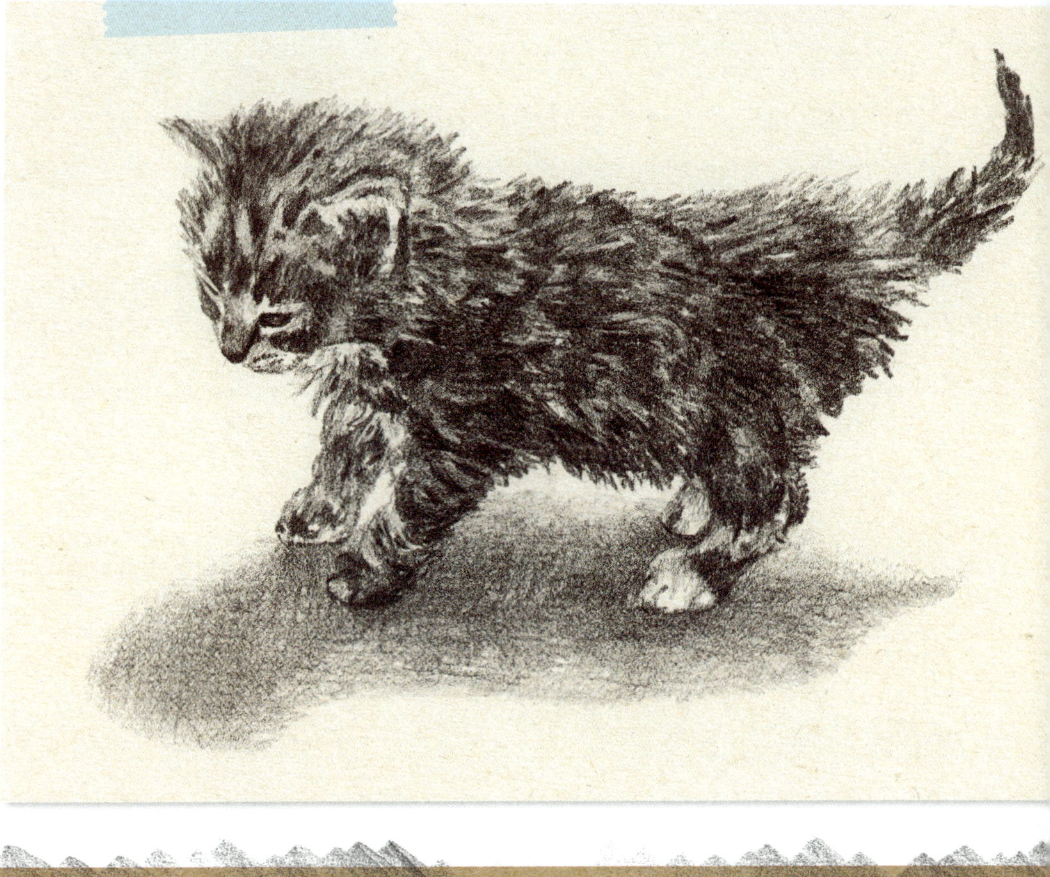

Going to the zoo is a great place to start drawing animals as well as a terrific day out. Take your visual diary to sketch in, and your camera so you can have a backup reference when you go home.

Try some of the animals that are fairly stationary first. Lions can be quite sleepy and will often stay still for lengths of time while you draw.

Following the same format as our other drawings, start by loosely sketching the shape, making sure the proportions look right. Add tone using a looser and more fluid style for the mane.

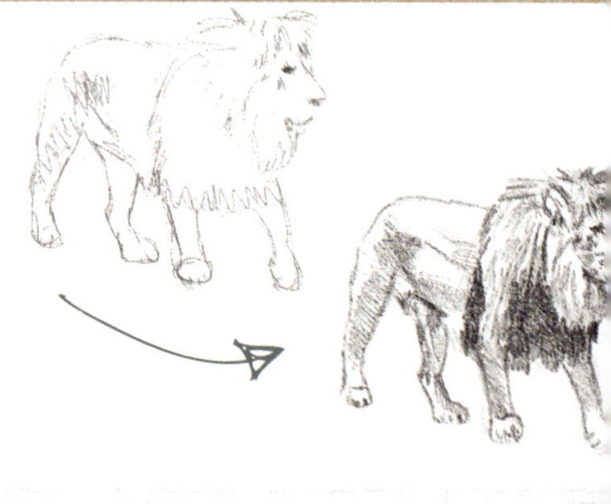

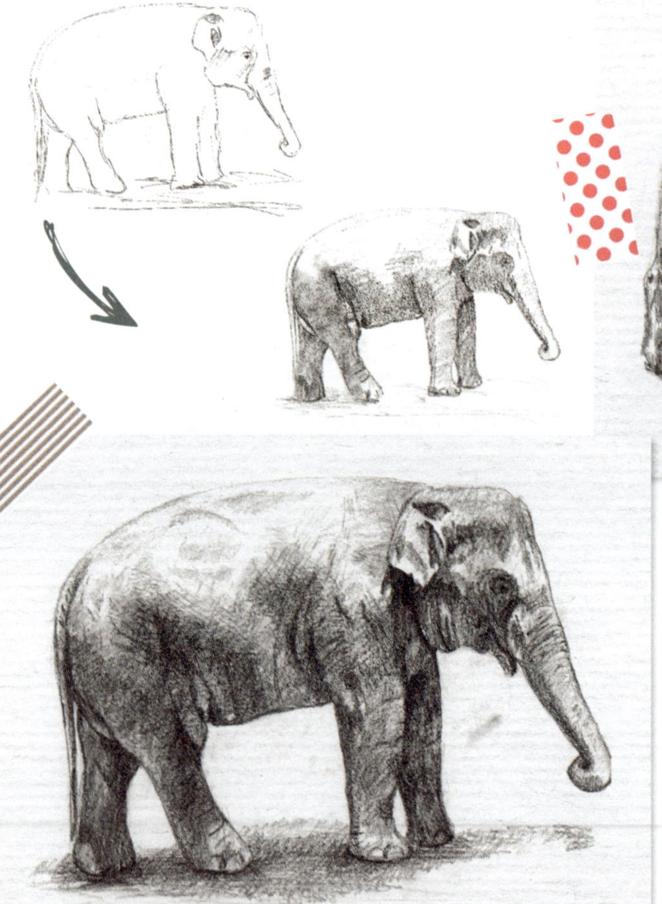

Elephants, with fabulous crevices and crinkles in their skin, are also great to draw.

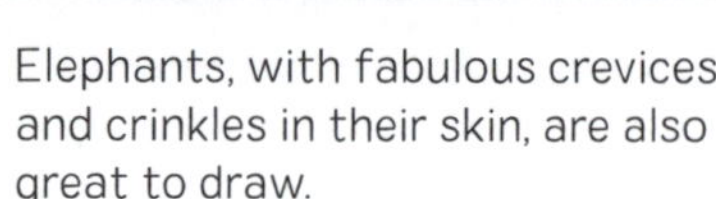

Once again, the general shape is sketched. Notice the proportion of the ears to the head and the layers of skin bordering the gentle eyes. Add tone, making sure that the crevices retain their form.

When you're at home, using a reference from books or photos can be great practice, giving you time to

Sketching where you go

Start taking your sketchbook out with you so you can jot down images whenever it takes your fancy – people, cars, animals ... anything! Your eyes are your best drawing tool, so put them to good use.

Practise drawing a whole variety of things, such as different leaves and flowers. Look at their distinctive shapes and details. It's the minutiae in all these objects that make them interesting.

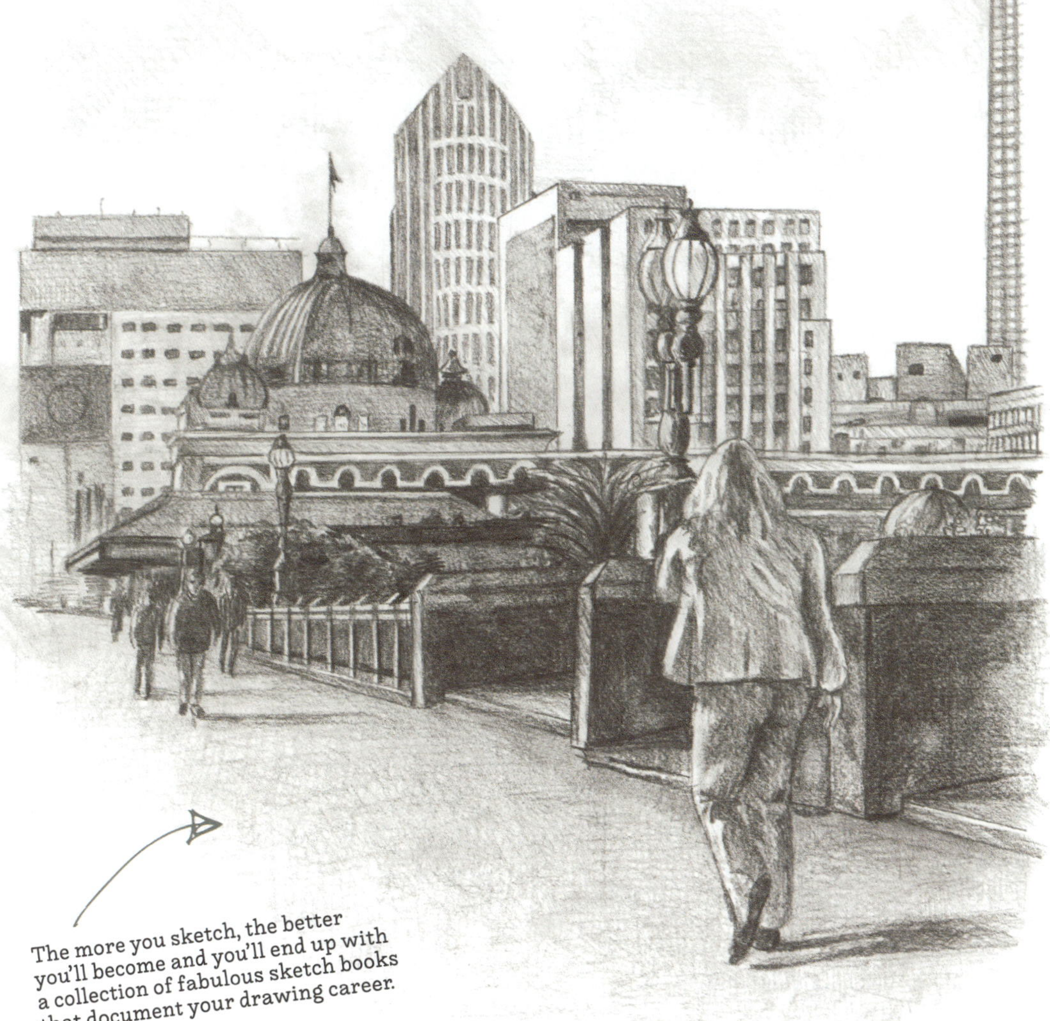

The more you sketch, the better you'll become and you'll end up with a collection of fabulous sketch books that document your drawing career.

Sketching challenges

In the following pages you will find a range of prompts for sketching a variety of aspects of your life. Sketch the **people** that are important to you, **animals** in your life, **places** you spend time at or wish to visit, **still life** items and objects that make up your living space and let your imagination run free by **doodling** patterns and images that come to you.

PEOPLE

WHO IS YOUR FAVOURITE PERSON ON THE ENTIRE PLANET?

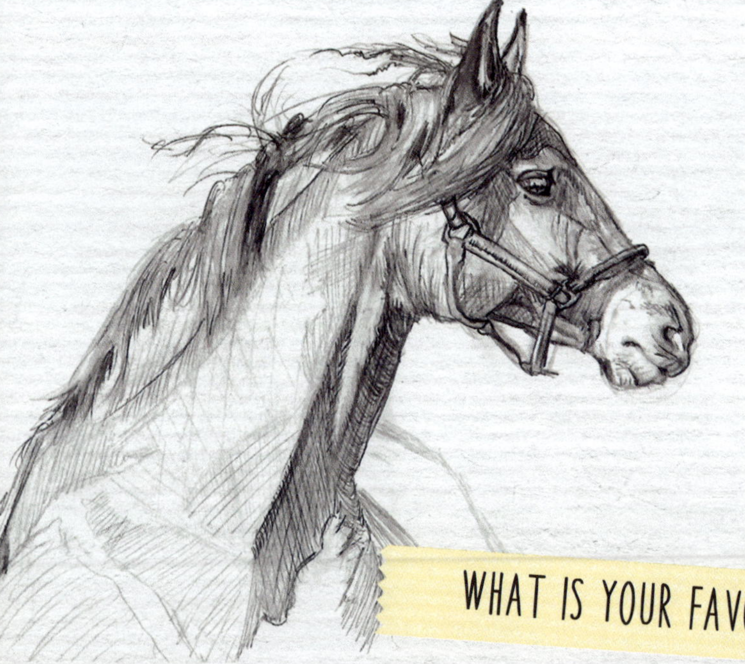

ANIMALS

WHAT IS YOUR FAVOURITE TYPE OF ANIMAL?

PLACES

WHERE ARE YOU RIGHT NOW?

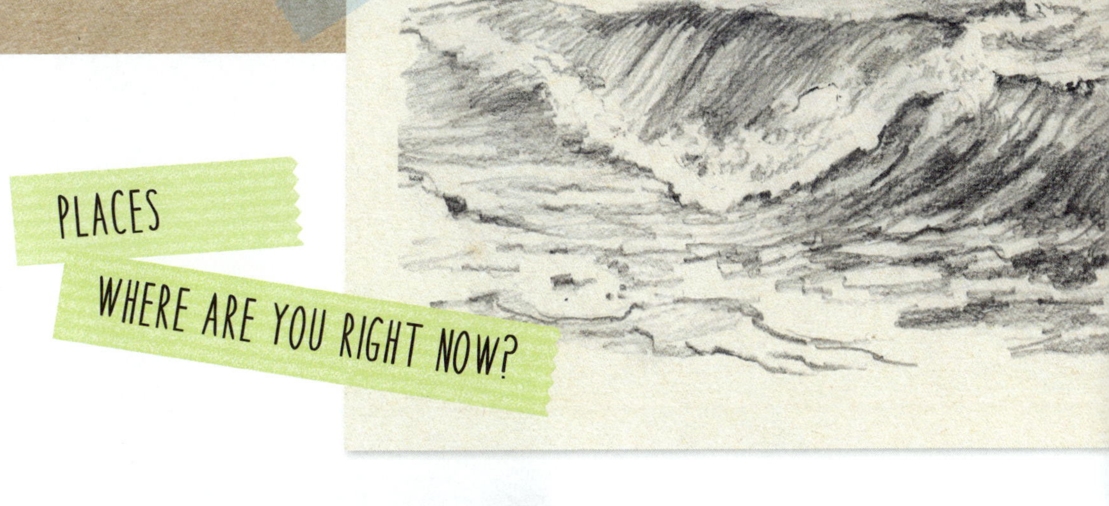

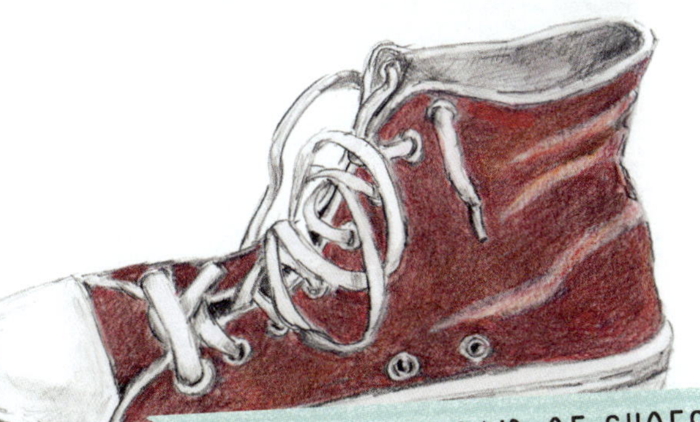

STILL LIFE

PICK OUT THE PAIR OF SHOES YOU WEAR THE MOST OFTEN...

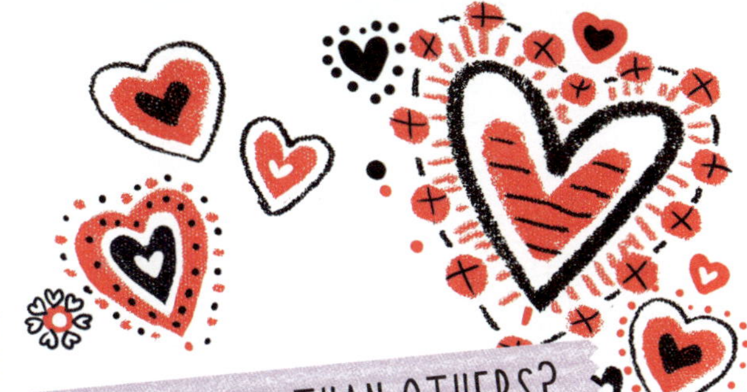

DOODLES

DO YOU HAVE A SHAPE YOU LIKE MORE THAN OTHERS?

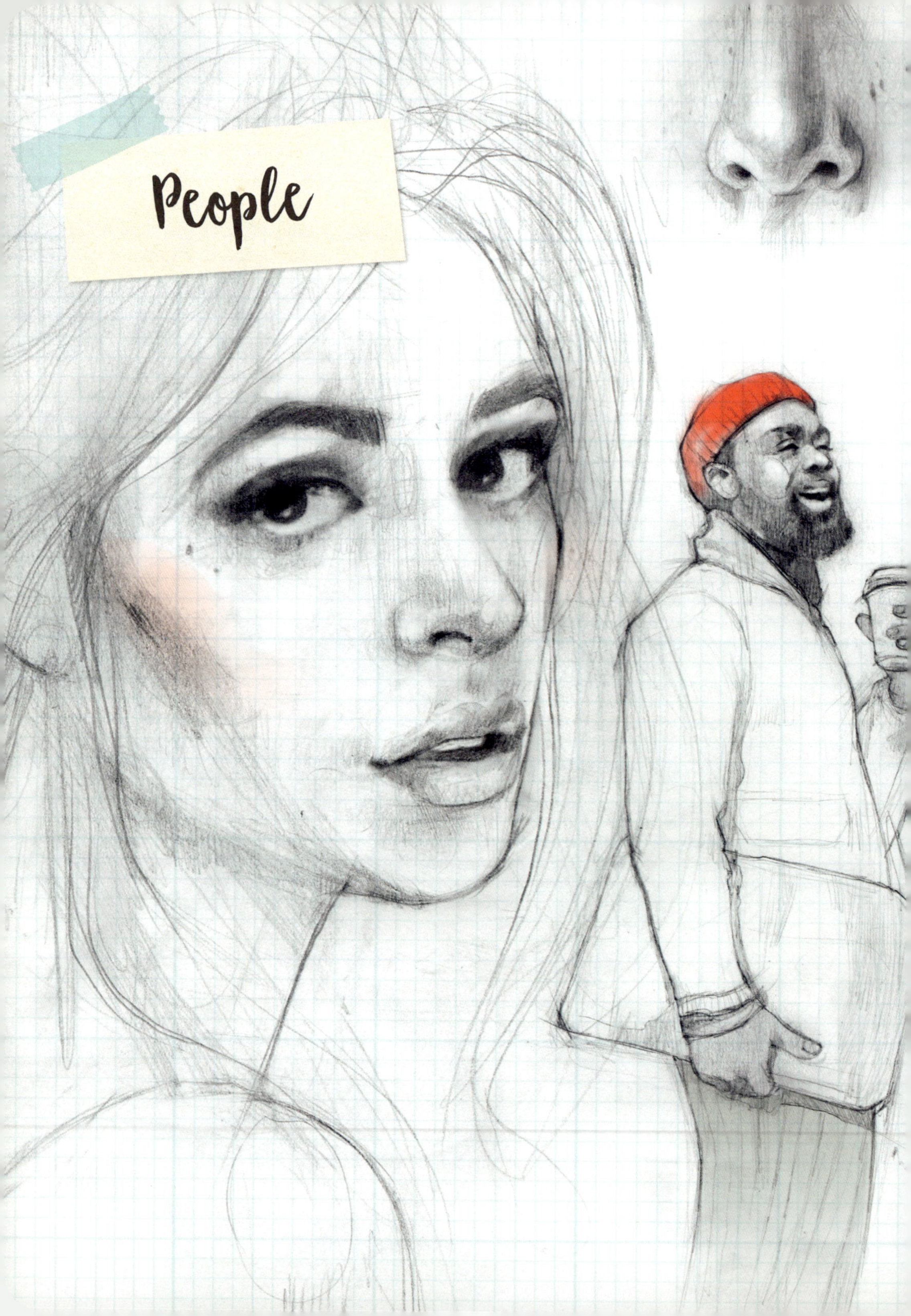
People

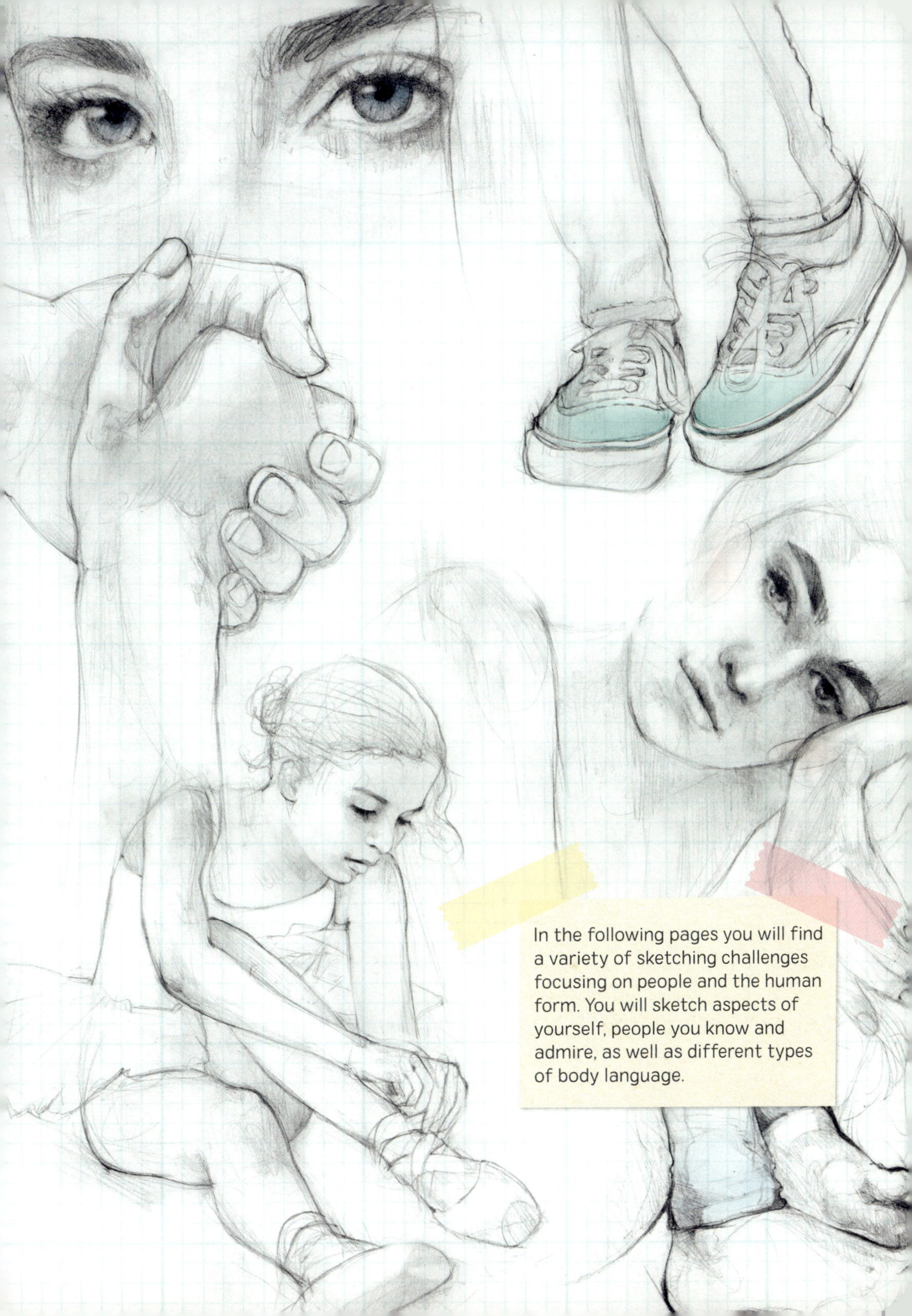

In the following pages you will find a variety of sketching challenges focusing on people and the human form. You will sketch aspects of yourself, people you know and admire, as well as different types of body language.

WHO ARE YOU?

What people, places, experiences, objects and passions make up you? Fill these pages with everything that makes you you.

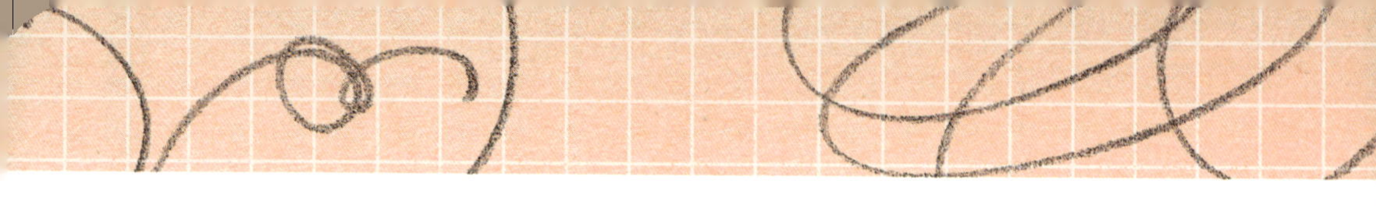

SIT IN FRONT OF A MIRROR.

Draw a self-portrait, but do not look down at your page.

SKETCH YOURSELF EXPRESSING

FOUR DIFFERENT EMOTIONS.

WHEN WAS THE LAST TIME YOU LOOKED CLOSELY AT A LOVED ONE?

Choose someone important to you and draw their best feature. Is it their smile? Their freckles? The way they carry themselves? Sketch your favourite thing about them here.

WHO IS YOUR FAVOURITE PERSON ON THE ENTIRE PLANET?

Is it your partner? Your best friend? Your little sister? A celebrity? Sketch them here.

SKETCH SOMEONE IN MOVEMENT.

Running, skipping, dancing, cheering. What are they doing?

DRAW SOMEONE SITTING IN CLASS OR A MEETING.

Imagine their body language, how they hold themselves at the start of the meeting and draw that. Now draw how they are sitting toward the end of the meeting. Do they look any different?

THINK OF A PERSON; ANY PERSON YOU LIKE (OR DISLIKE!)

Draw them as an infant, a teen, an adult and a senior citizen.

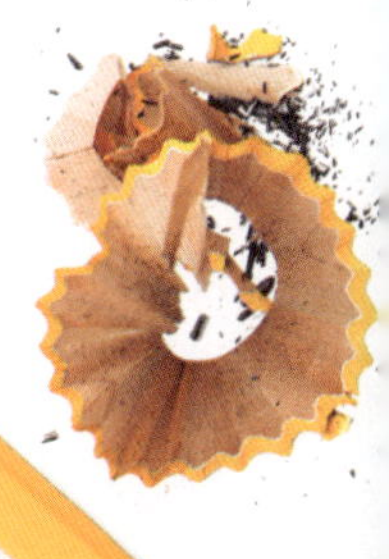

Now it's your turn! Practise your favourite of the sketching prompts again or try out a new technique here.

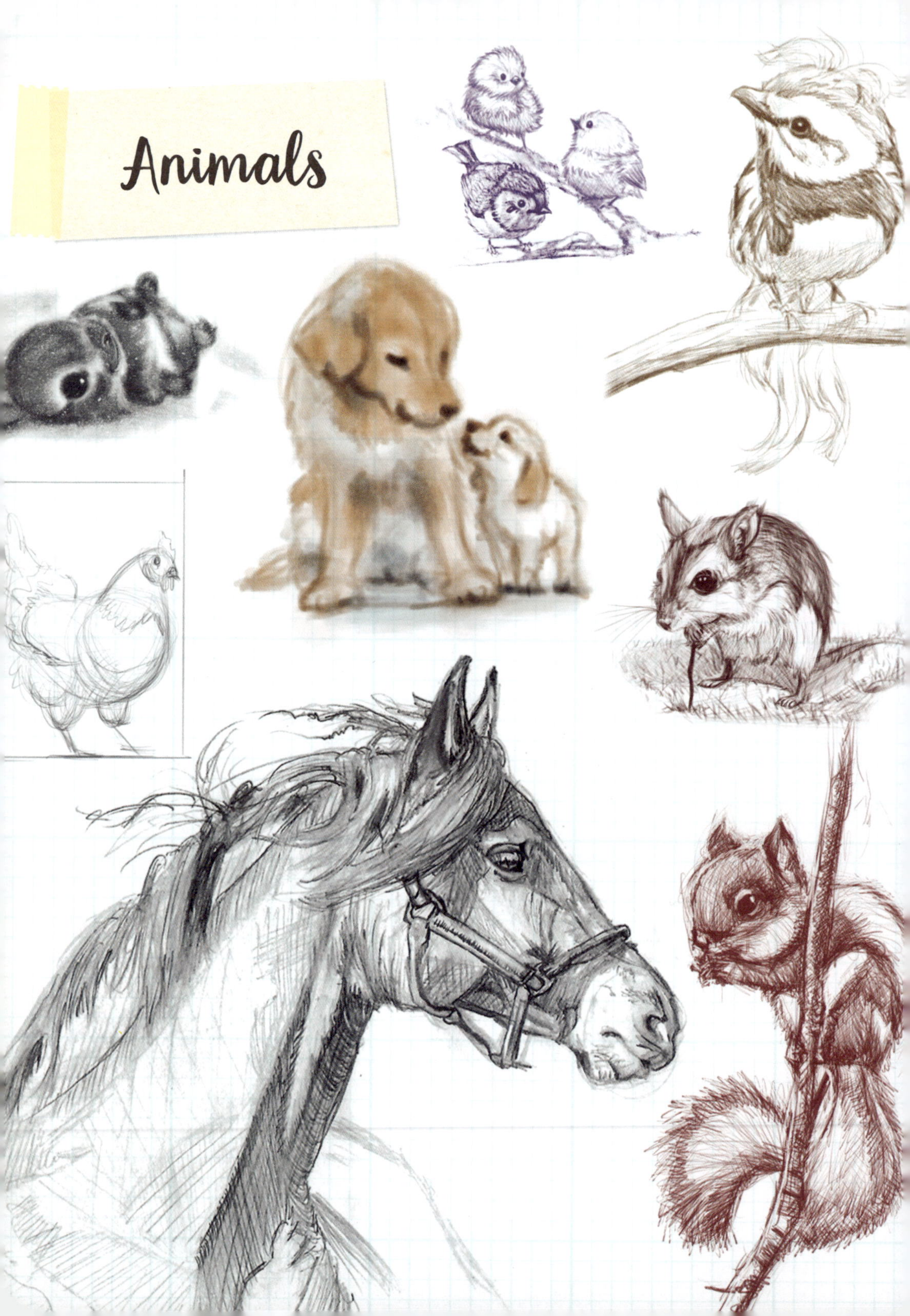
Animals

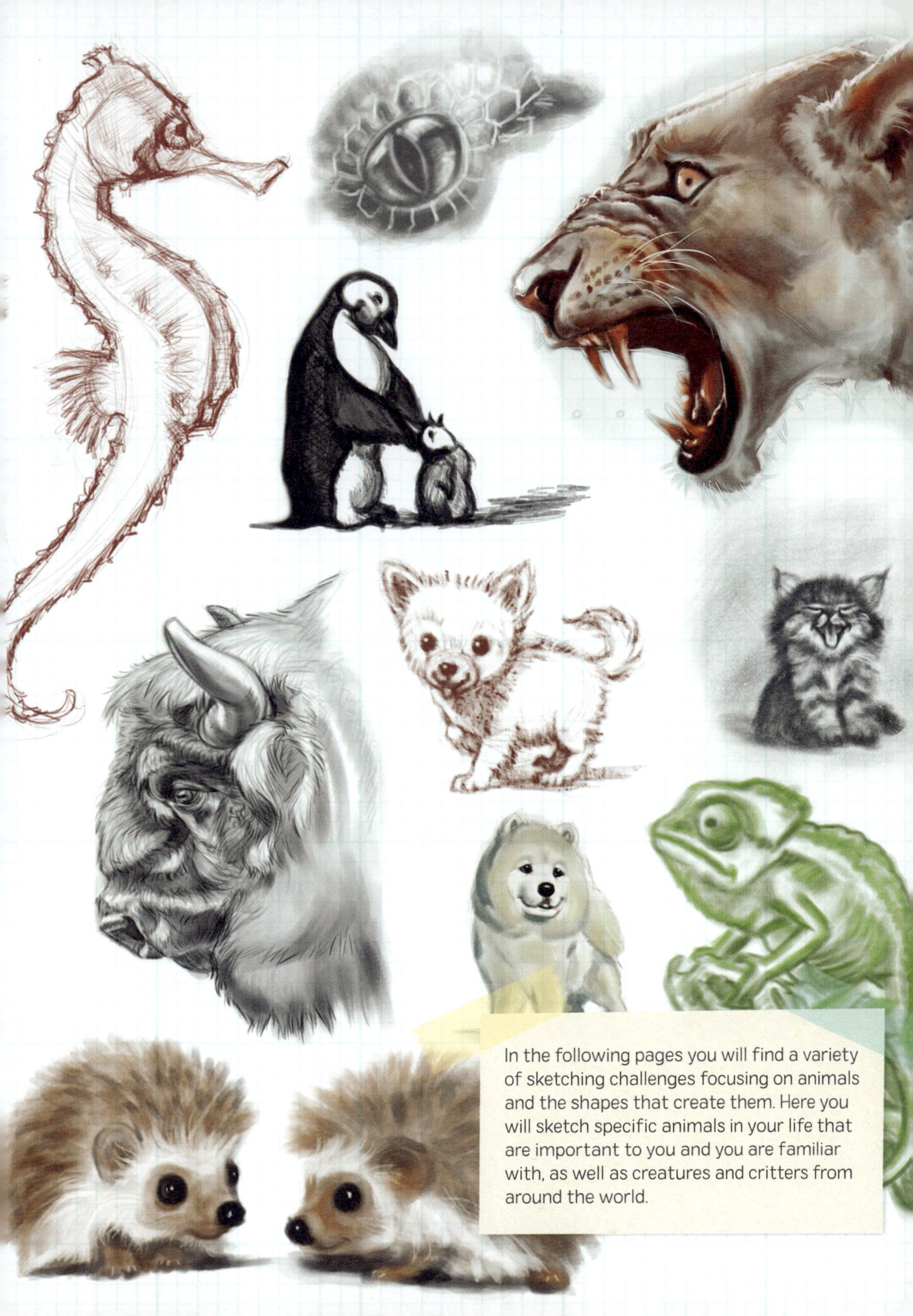

In the following pages you will find a variety of sketching challenges focusing on animals and the shapes that create them. Here you will sketch specific animals in your life that are important to you and you are familiar with, as well as creatures and critters from around the world.

DESIGN YOURSELF AS AN ANIMAL.

Are you a good listener so would have big, floppy ears like an elephant? Are you a fast runner so would have the sleek body of a cheetah? What animalistic features would you have?

SKETCH AN ANIMAL THAT MEANS A LOT TO YOU.

Is your pet dog your best friend? Does the cat that lives down the street warm your heart?

WHAT IS YOUR FAVOURITE TYPE OF ANIMAL IN THE WORLD?

Draw it here.

NOW DRAW YOUR FAVOURITE

ANIMAL AGAIN WITH ONE LINE...

DON'T LIFT YOUR PEN FROM THE PAGE.

ARE YOU RIGHT-HANDED?

CHOOSE AN ANIMAL

AND QUICKLY DRAW IT WITH YOUR LEFT HAND.

If you're left-handed, draw with your right hand, but do it quickly!

This activity challenges you to loosen up your creative brain and let go of striving for perfection.

Your sketches won't be perfect – and that's great.

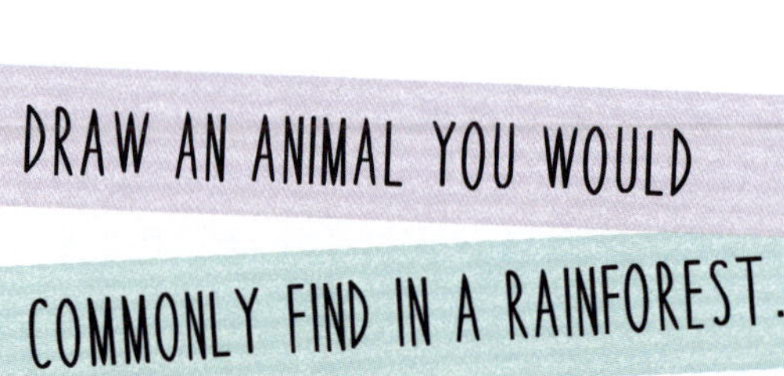
DRAW AN ANIMAL YOU WOULD
COMMONLY FIND IN A RAINFOREST.

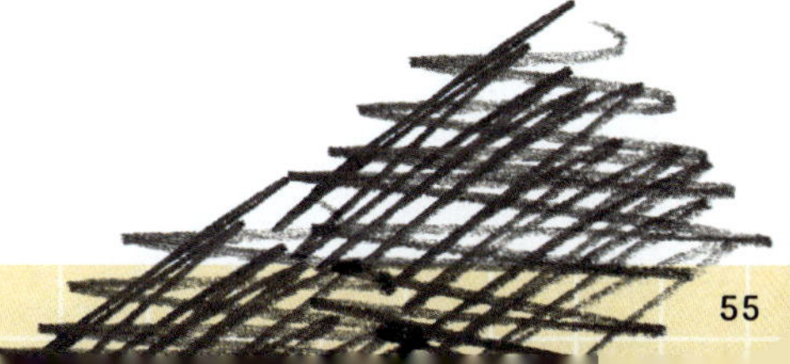

DRAW FURRY AND FLUFFY, SILKY AND SCALY ANIMAL FACES!

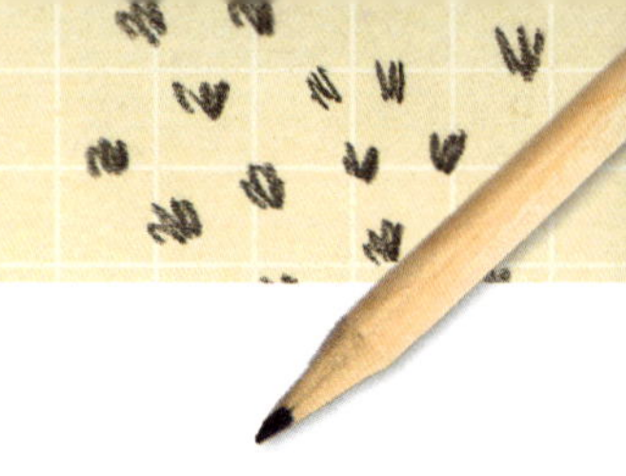

Sketch a dog, cat, rabbit, ferret, mouse, snake, iguana and fish on these pages.

THINK OF A HORSE GALLOPING.

What shapes can you see that show the horse in motion? Draw the horse with as few lines as possible.

FILL THE PAGE WITH GREY.

Rub the page with the side of a soft grey lead pencil (about 6B). With an eraser, lift off the grey lead to create an illustration of an animal. This technique is called negative drawing.

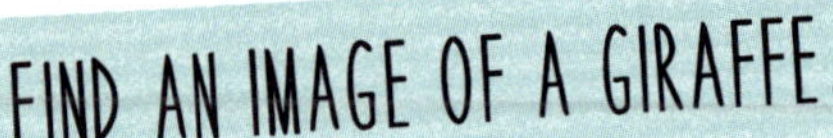

Look at the giraffe and draw it upside down.

NOW FLIP THE IMAGE UPSIDE DOWN AND DRAW THE GIRAFFE RIGHT-WAY UP.

DO YOUR GIRAFFES LOOK DIFFERENT?

USING LOTS OF SHORT LINES, DRAW A LION.

Give its mane longer lines to create longer hairs.

ANIMALS ARE MADE OUT OF DIFFERENT SHAPES WHEN THEY ARE AT REST OR IN MOTION.

Watch your pet or find an animal and analyse the different shapes that they are made up of in different movements.

With straight lines for speed, curved lines for climbing, etc., sketch the animals of your choice in a variety of movements.

Now it's your turn!

Practise your favourite of the sketching prompts again or try out a new technique here.

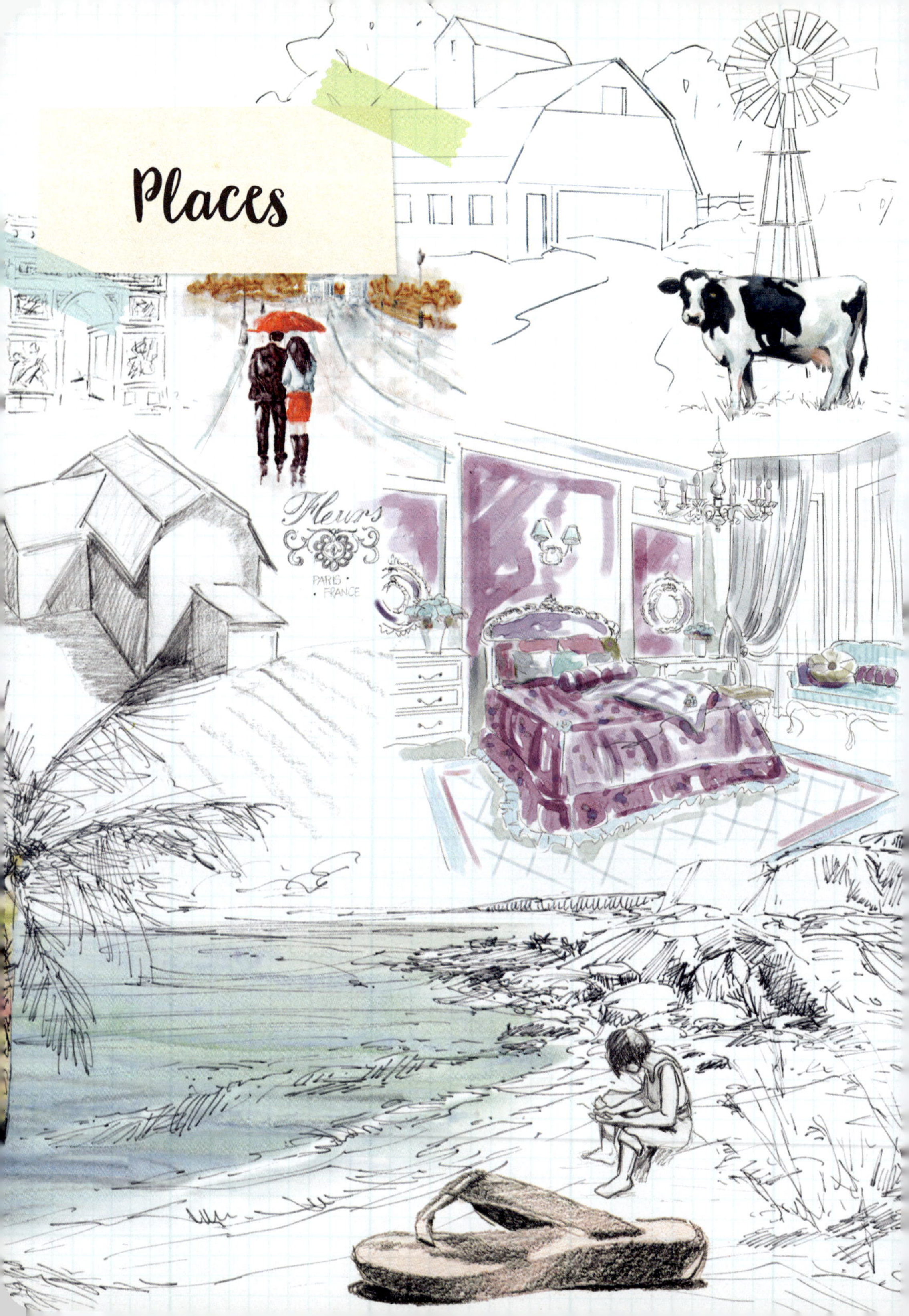
Places
Fleurs
PARIS
FRANCE

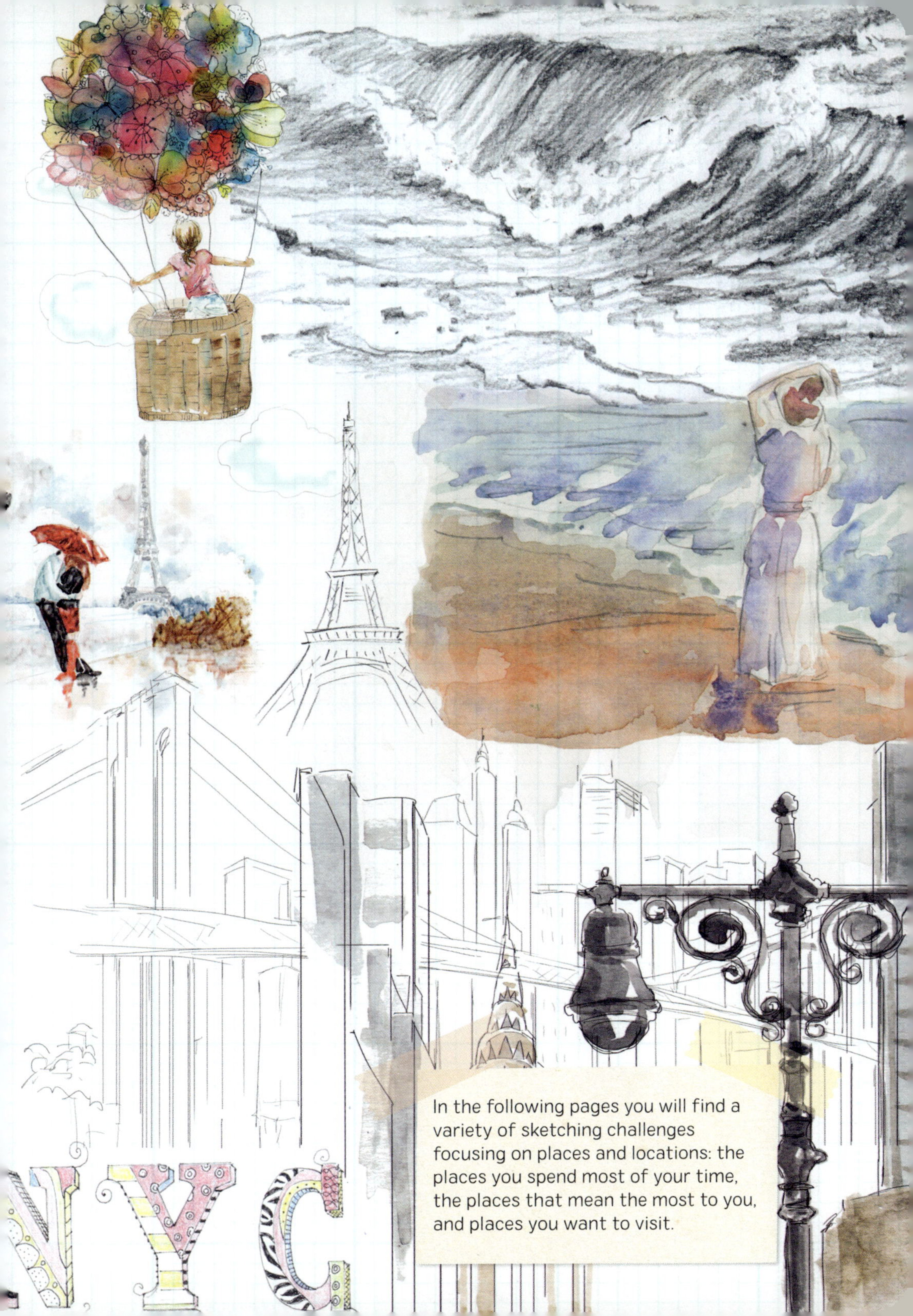

In the following pages you will find a variety of sketching challenges focusing on places and locations: the places you spend most of your time, the places that mean the most to you, and places you want to visit.

CLOSE YOUR EYES AND THINK OF YOUR IDEAL PLACE.

What do you see? Sketch it here, but keep your eyes closed!

NOW SKETCH IT AGAIN HERE

WITH YOUR EYES OPEN.

DRAW WHERE YOU LIVE.

Do you live in a house or an apartment? Is it modern or rustic? Clean and tidy or worn and lived-in? Sketch where you live here.

LOOK OUT A WINDOW NEAR YOU.

SKETCH WHAT'S OUTSIDE.

WHAT IS IT LIKE IN THE TOWN WHERE YOU LIVE?

SKETCH IT HERE.

DRAW YOUR FAVOURITE PLACES

IN THE TOWN OR CITY YOU LIVE IN.

SKETCH A FEW PLACES YOU'VE BEEN.

DRAW SOME PLACES YOU WOULD LIKE TO TRAVEL TO.

THINK ABOUT WHAT IMAGES REPRESENT EACH SEASON.

Sketch the seasons here.

CLOSE YOUR EYES

AND IMAGINE A MOUNTAIN.

Is it a mountain range? Thick with forest, or perhaps covered in snow? Without opening your eyes, sketch what you see here.

THE OCEAN LOOKS DIFFERENT AT DIFFERENT TIMES OF DAY AND IN DIFFERENT WEATHER.

Do you prefer high tide or low tide with vast sandy beaches? Perhaps you prefer calm beaches, choppy water during a storm or towering waves perfect for surfing on a sunny day.

Use these pages to sketch your perfect beach scene.

Now it's your turn!

Practise your favourite of the sketching prompts again or try out a new technique here.

Still Life

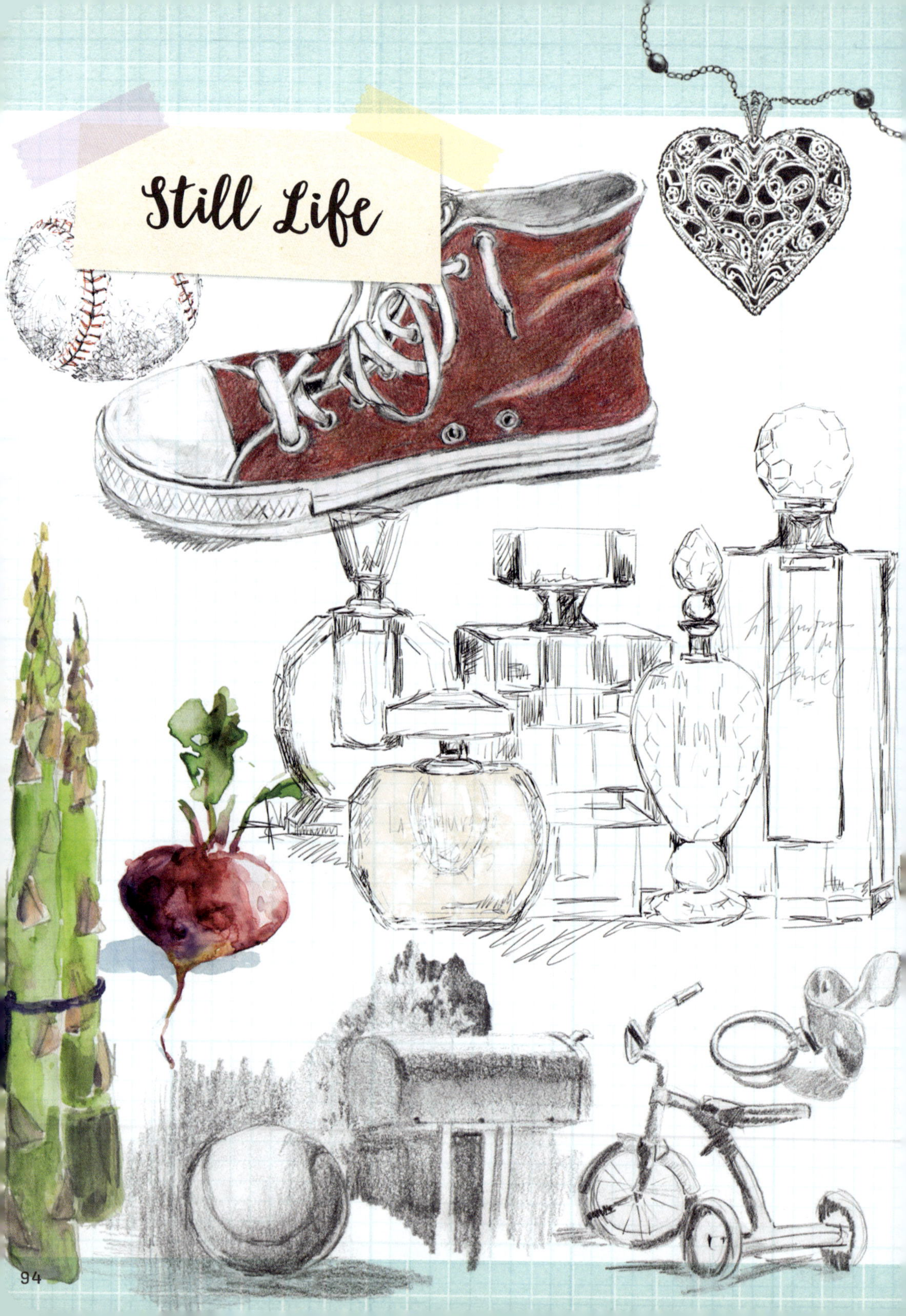

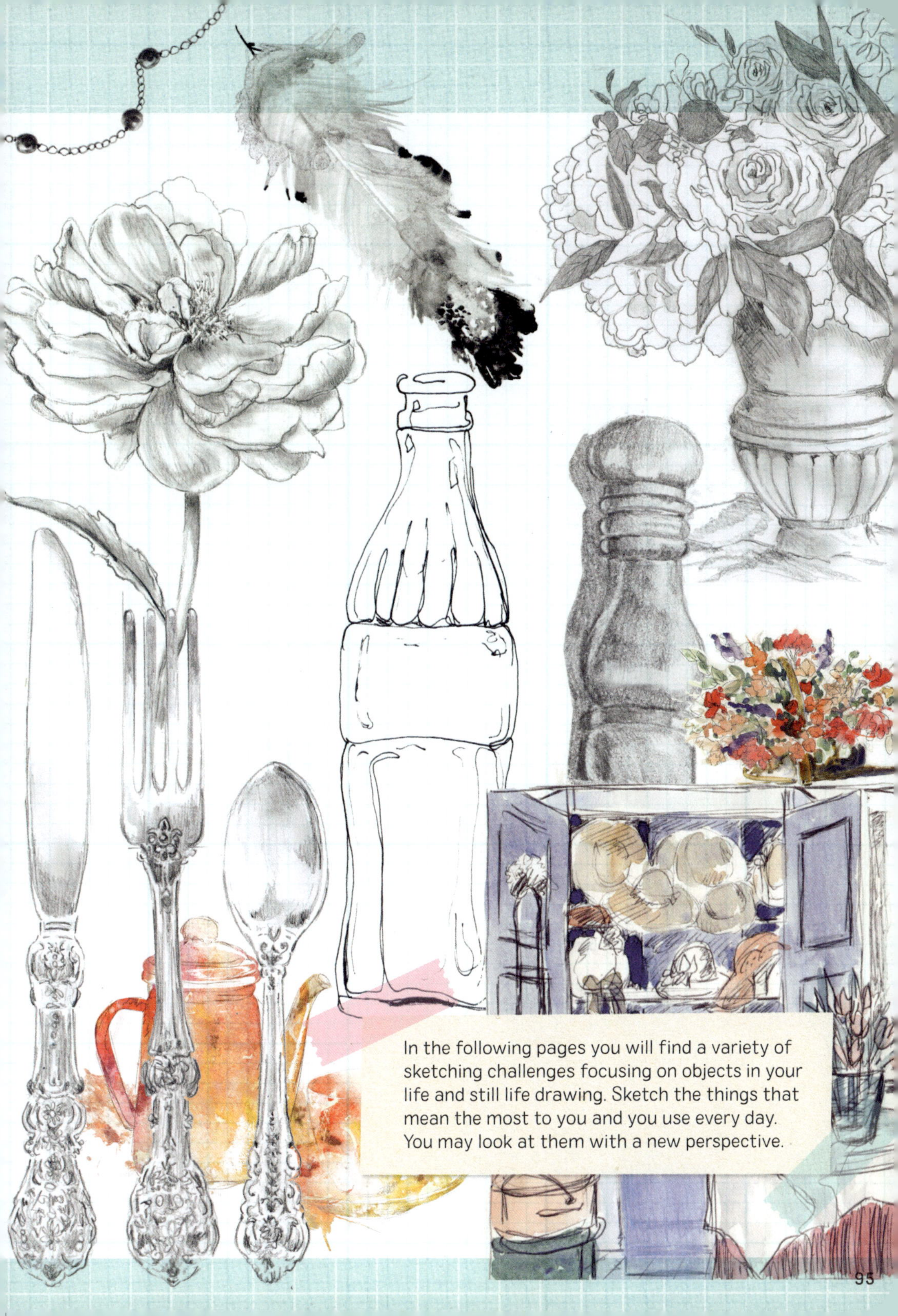

In the following pages you will find a variety of sketching challenges focusing on objects in your life and still life drawing. Sketch the things that mean the most to you and you use every day. You may look at them with a new perspective.

WHAT ARE SOME THINGS YOU USE EVERY DAY?

Do you drink a mug of coffee? Read a book? Watch TV? Do you wear the same piece of jewellery every day? Sketch your everyday items here.

WHAT IS YOUR FAVOURITE MEAL OR MEALS?

Draw the most delicious foods you can think of here.

SKETCH YOUR TOOTHBRUSH...

USING ONLY ONE LINE.

PICK AN OBJECT AND DO

A LINE DRAWING OF IT.

NOW DRAW IT AGAIN BUT ADD SHADING.

THINK OF AN OBJECT THAT MEANS A LOT TO YOU.

Draw it here from memory.

GET THE OBJECT AND DRAW IT
AGAIN WITH IT IN FRONT OF YOU.

ARRANGE SOME FRUIT AND VEGETABLES ON A DISH.

Sketch a classic piece of still life art.

SELECT AN OBJECT WITH FOUR SIDES.

DRAW EACH SIDE INDIVIDUALLY.

SCRUNCH UP A PIECE OF PAPER AND DRAW WHAT YOU SEE.

Include shadows and contours of the page.

POUR YOURSELF A GLASS OF WATER AND REALLY LOOK AT IT.

Draw reflections and light refractions and everything you can see.

RETRIEVE THE PAIR OF SHOES YOU WEAR THE MOST OFTEN AND SKETCH THEM HERE.

Now it's your turn!

Practise your favourite of the sketching prompts again or try out a new technique here.

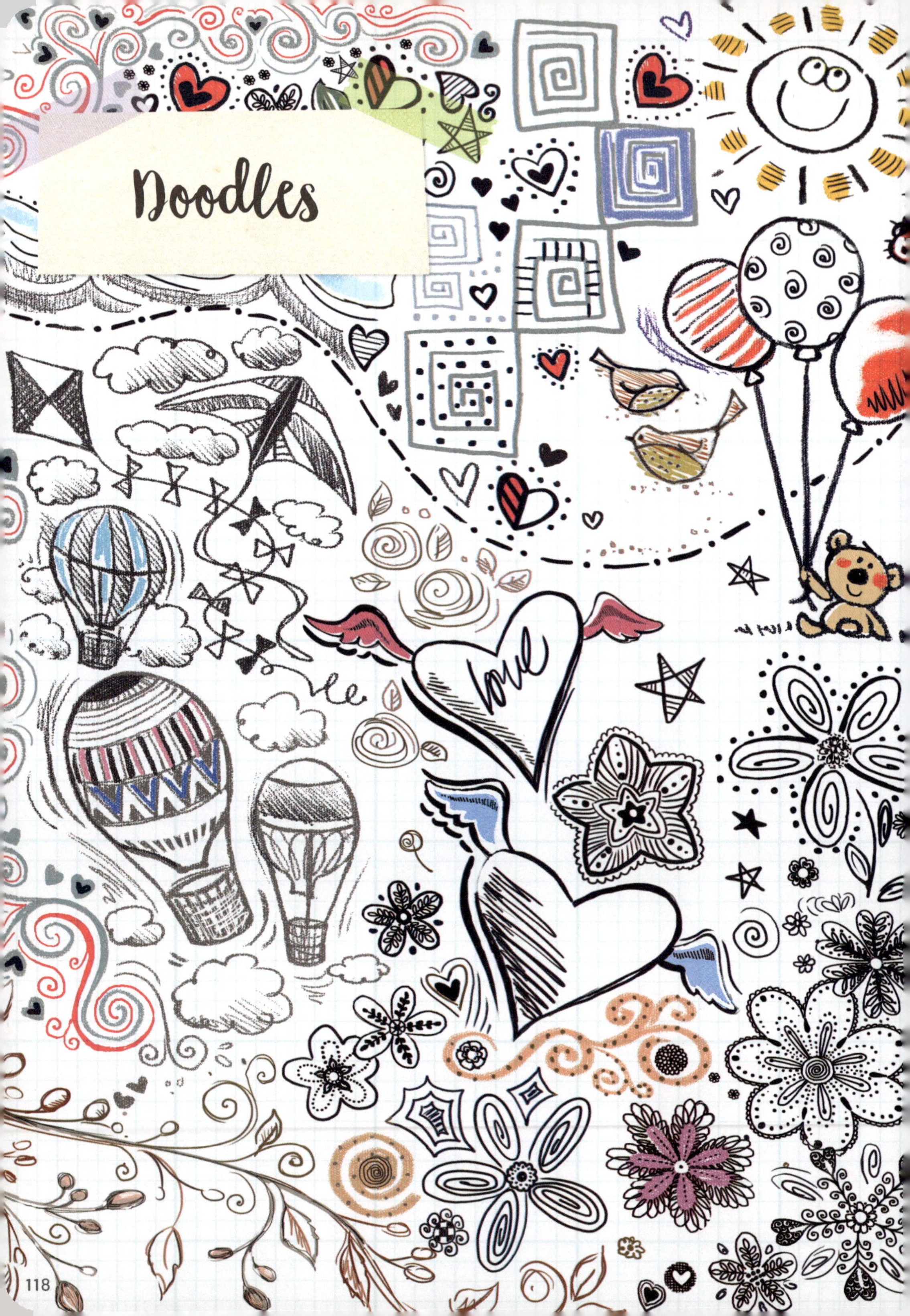
Doodles
love

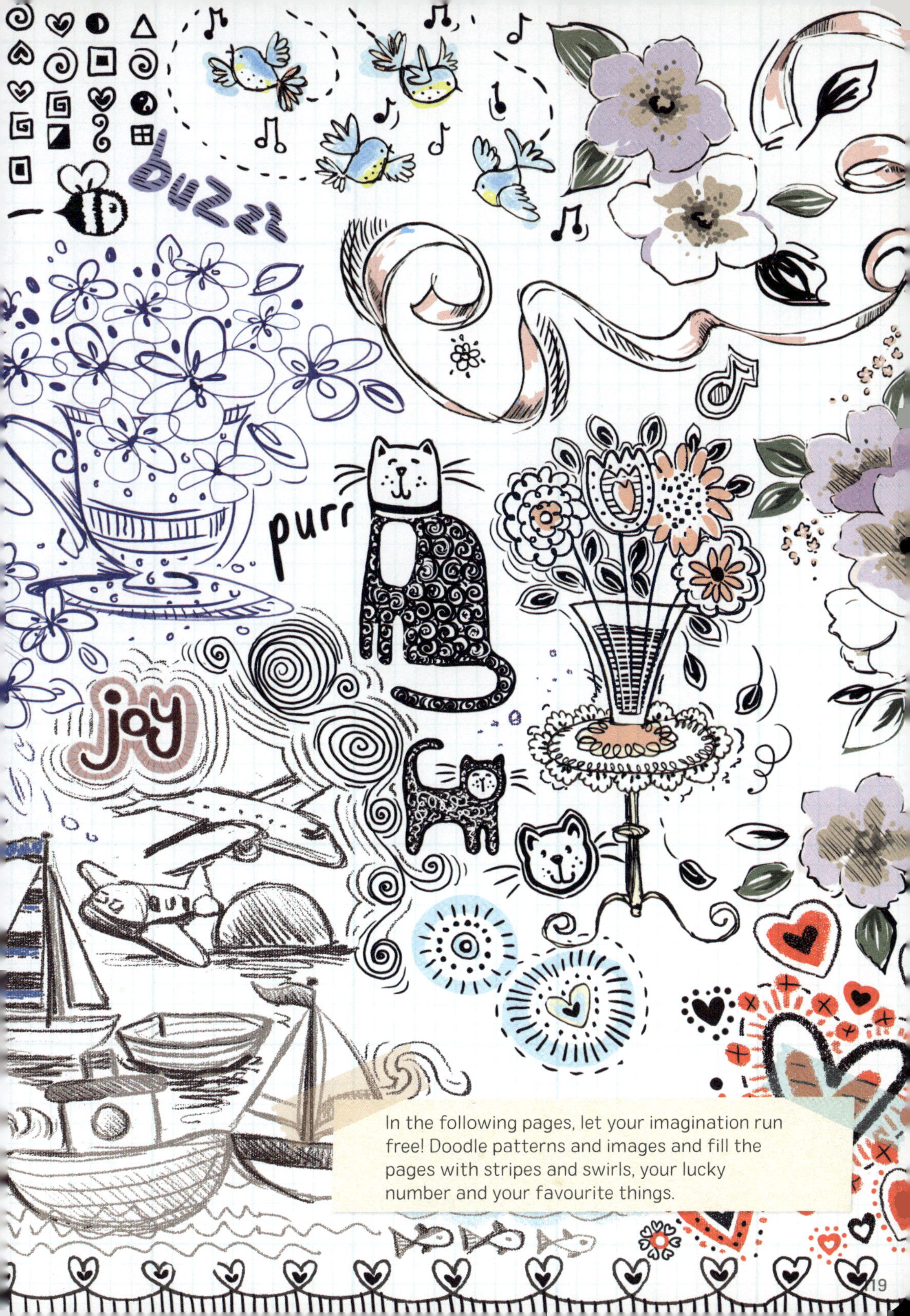

In the following pages, let your imagination run free! Doodle patterns and images and fill the pages with stripes and swirls, your lucky number and your favourite things.

DO YOU HAVE A SHAPE YOU LIKE MORE THAN OTHERS?

Do you like hard edges and corners of squares, diamonds and stars, or do you prefer soft shapes like circles, ovals and hearts? Fill the page with your favourite shape – but don't lift your pen from the page.

WHAT ARE SOME THINGS THAT MAKE YOU HAPPY?

Do you like a good cup of coffee? A warm, sunny day? Perhaps you have a favourite ring or TV show. Maybe you love the first snowflake of the year. Cover the page with doodles that represent all the things that make you happy.

DO YOU HAVE A LUCKY NUMBER?

What is the number that means the most to you? Fill the page with as many different things as you can think of that contain or represent your lucky number.

PICK A WORD, ANY WORD!

Which word came to mind first? What shapes, patterns and images represent it? Fill the page with representations of your word.

SWIRLS AND CURLY LINES ARE A CLASSIC FORM OF DOODLING.

Place your pen or pencil on the page and don't lift it until you have filled as much as you can with swirls and curls.

WHAT KIND OF PATTERNS CAN YOU CREATE ONLY USING STRAIGHT LINES?

FILL FIVE BOXES WITH FIVE DIFFERENT PATTERNS.

Now continue those patterns to form a patchwork all the way down the pages.

HOW ARE YOU FEELING TODAY?

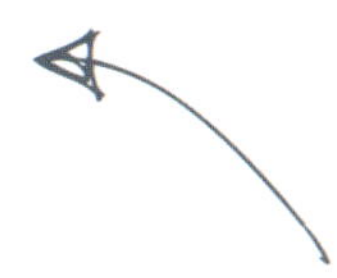

DOODLE IT HERE.

DO YOU LIKE DAFFODILS?

PERHAPS YOUR FAVOURITE FLOWERS ARE TULIPS.

Fill the page with as many flowers as you can think of.

Now it's your turn!

Practise your favourite of the sketching prompts again or try out a new technique here.

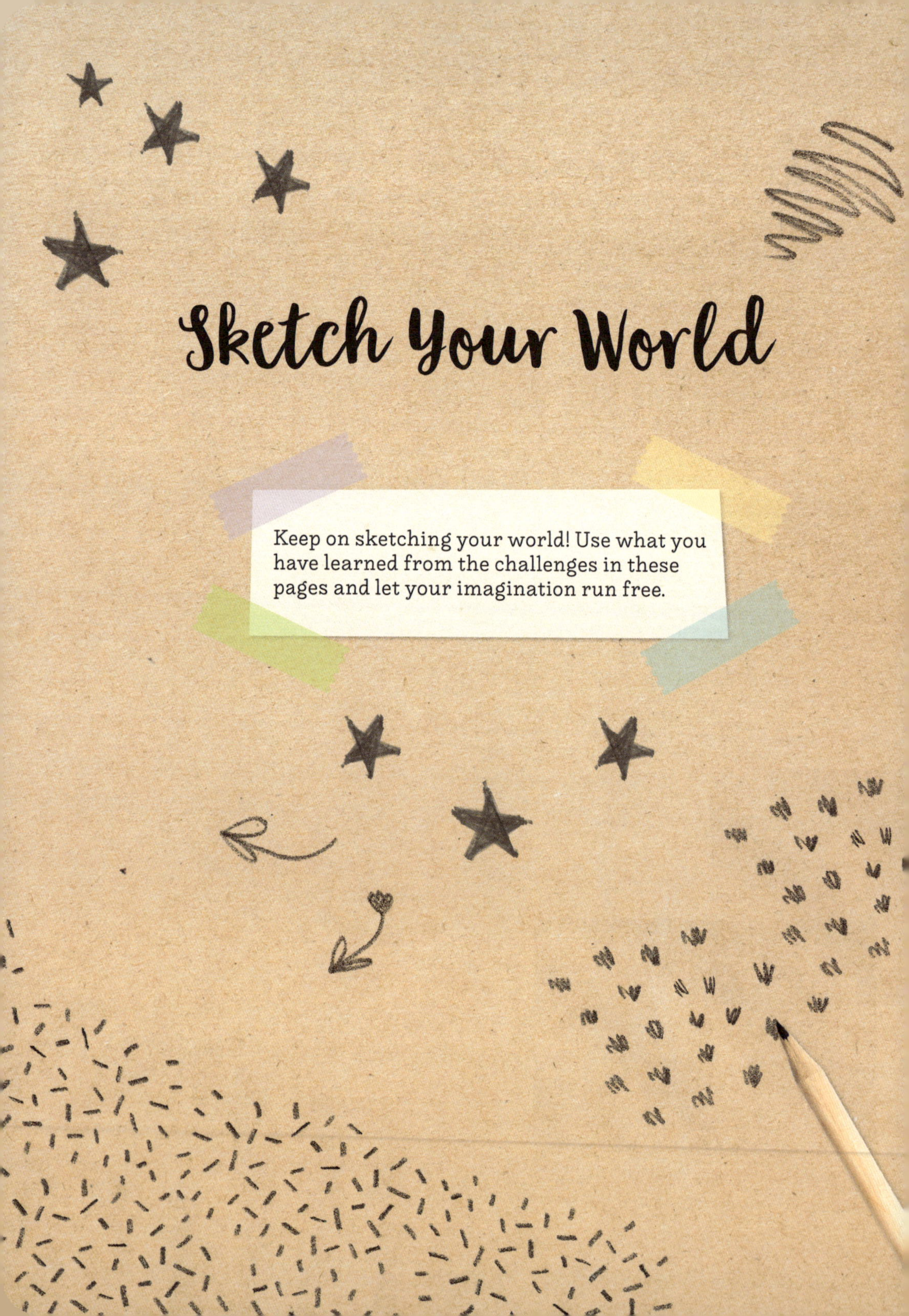

Sketch Your World

Keep on sketching your world! Use what you have learned from the challenges in these pages and let your imagination run free.

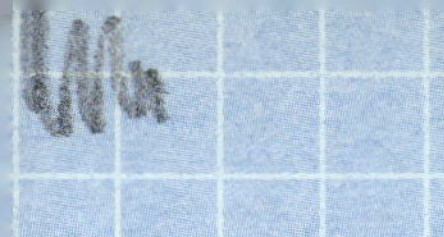

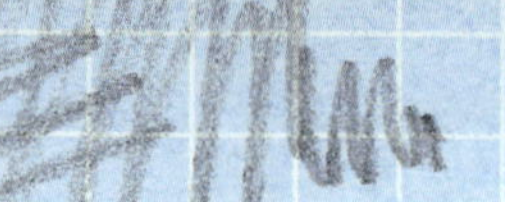

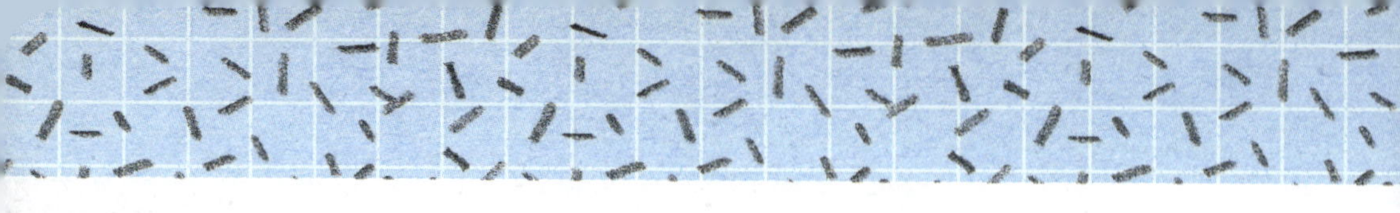